KU-107-224

C A P S T O N E

Stay Smart!

Smart things to know about... is a complete library of the world's smartest business ideas. **Smart** books put you on the inside track to the knowledge and skills that make the most successful people tick.

Each book brings you right up to speed on a crucial business issue. The subjects that business people tell us they most want to master are:

Smart Things to Know about **Brands & Branding**, JOHN MARIOTTI
Smart Things to Know about **Business Finance**, KEN LANGDON
Smart Things to Know about **Change**, DAVID FIRTH
Smart Things to Know about **CRM**, DAVID HARVEY
Smart Things to Know about **Customers**, ROS JAY
Smart Things to Know about **Decision Making**, KEN LANGDON

Smart Things to Know about **E-Business**, MICHAEL J. CUNNINGHAM
Smart Things to Know about **E-Commerce**, MICHAEL J. CUNNINGHAM
Smart Things to Know about **Growth**, TONY GRUNDY
Smart Things to Know about **Innovation & Creativity**, DENNIS SHERWOOD
Smart Things to Know about **Knowledge Management**,
TOM M. KOULOPOULOS & CARL FRAPPAOLO

Smart Things to Know about **Leadership**,
JONATHAN YUDELOWITZ, RICHARD KOCH & ROBIN FIELD
Smart Things to Know about **Managing Projects**, DONNA DEEPROSE
Smart Things to Know about **Marketing**, JOHN MARIOTTI
Smart Things to Know about **Partnerships**, JOHN MARIOTTI
Smart Things to Know about **People Management**, DAVID FIRTH

Smart Things to Know about **Scenario Planning**, TONY KIPPENBERGER
Smart Things to Know about **Strategy**, RICHARD KOCH
Smart Things to Know about **Teams**, ANNEMARIE CARACCIOLO
Smart Things to Know about **Your Career**, JOHN MIDDLETON

You can stay **Smart** by e-mailing us at **info@wiley-capstone.co.uk**
Let us keep you up to date with new Smart books, Smart updates, a Smart newsletter
and Smart seminars and conferences. Get in touch to discuss your needs.

CAPSTONE

Smart

THINGS TO KNOW ABOUT

Motivation

DONNA DEEPROSE

Copyright © Donna Deeprose 2003

The right of Donna Deeprose to be identified as the author of this book has been asserted in accordance with the Copyright, Designs and Patents Act 1988

First Published 2003 by
Capstone Publishing Limited (a Wiley company)
8 Newtec Place
Magdalen Road
Oxford
OX4 1RE
United Kingdom
http://www.capstoneideas.com

All Rights Reserved. Except for the quotation of small passages for the purposes of criticism and review, no part of this publication may be reproduced, stored in a retrieval system or transmitted in any form or by any means, electronic, mechanical, photocopying, recording, scanning or otherwise, except under the terms of the Copyright, Designs and Patents Act 1988 or under the terms of a licence issued by the Copyright Licensing Agency Ltd, 90 Tottenham Court Road, London W1T 4LP, UK, without the permission in writing of the Publisher. Requests to the Publisher should be addressed to the Permissions Department, John Wiley & Sons Ltd, The Atrium, Southern Gate, Chichester, West Sussex, PO19 8SQ, England, or emailed to permreq@wiley.co.uk, or faxed to (+44) 1243 770571.

CIP catalogue records for this book are available from the British Library and the US Library of Congress

ISBN 1-84112-417-6

Typeset in 11/15pt Sabon by Sparks Computer Solutions Ltd, Oxford, UK (http://www.sparks.co.uk)
Printed and bound by T.J. International Ltd, Padstow, Cornwall

Substantial discounts on bulk quantities of Capstone Books are available to corporations, professional associations and other organizations. For details telephone Capstone Publishing on (+44-1865-798623), fax (+44-1865-240941) or email (info@wiley-capstone.co.uk)

Contents

Acknowledgments

Many people shared their knowledge and experiences with me so that I could bring this book to life. I contacted a number of acknowledged experts whose own related books taught me much; and in conversations, they taught me even more. They included Jon Katzenbach, Mike Maccoby, Ken Thomas and Hank Karp. People like Joe Meilan, Cheryl Lazzaro, Patti Dowse and Florence Stone described corporate experiences and offered good advice arising from those. There's a group of consultants I call on regularly because I trust their guidance, people like Bill Becker, Rosalind Gold and Karen Massoni, whose input appears throughout the book. And there are people who talked freely, but preferred to remain anonymous. Thanks to all of you. I needed you all.

What is Smart?

The *Smart* series is a new way of learning. *Smart* books will improve your understanding and performance in some of the critical areas you face today like *customers, strategy, change, e-commerce, brands, influencing skills, knowledge management, finance, teamworking, partnerships.*

Smart books summarize accumulated wisdom as well as providing original cutting-edge ideas and tools that will take you out of theory and into action.

The widely respected business guru Chris Argyris points out that even the most intelligent individuals can become ineffective in organizations. Why? Because we are so busy working that we fail to learn about ourselves. We stop reflecting on the changes around us. We get sucked into the patterns of behaviour that have produced success for us in the past, not realizing that it may no longer be appropriate for us in the fast-approaching future.

There are three ways the *Smart* series helps prevent this happening to you:

- by increasing your self awareness;

- by developing your understanding, attitude and behaviour; and

- by giving you the tools to challenge the status quo that exists in your organization.

Smart people need smart organizations. You could spend a third of your career hopping around in search of the Holy Grail, or you could begin to create your own smart organization around you today.

Finally, a reminder that books don't change the world, people do. And although the *Smart* series offers you the brightest wisdom from the best practitioners and thinkers, these books throw the responsibility on you to *apply* what you're learning to your work.

Because the truly smart person knows that reading a book is the start of the process and not the end ...

As Eric Hoffer says, 'In times of change, learners inherit the world, while the learned remain beautifully equipped to deal with a world that no longer exists.'

David Firth
Smartmaster

Introduction

How many times have you heard gripes like these (or even muttered them yourself)?

- 'People just aren't motivated the way they used to be.' Of course, people have been saying that for hundreds, even thousands, of years.

- 'These young people expect to do it all before they're 30.' Hmm, somebody must be motivated.

- 'Workers here never take initiative. They don't do anything they aren't specifically instructed to do.' From managers.

- 'I used to make suggestions for improving things, but nobody listened. So now I just do what they say.' From employees.

- 'I don't care so much about the money, but it would be nice to get some appreciation.'

- 'Just give me the money. You can't pay the rent with thank-yous.'

Smart quotes

'When was the last time you heard someone say "Thank God it's Monday"?'

Dean R. Spitzer, *Supermotivation*[1]

It's all so confusing. So many contradictory observations, complaints, accusations and words of advice. Are people really less motivated to work than they used to be, or are they in a rush to do everything at once? Do workers refuse to take an extra step (let alone go an extra mile) or are managers holding them back by ignoring employees' good ideas? Is money a motivator or not?

Actually, the answers are yes, yes, yes, yes and yes – at different times, in different situations, with different people. There's no one-size-fits-all motivation. If you are a manager, you probably worked hard, overcame obstacles and stacked up achievements to get where you are. The irony is that whatever drove you to do that may be unimportant to some of the people who work for you. That doesn't mean they have no motivation; it just means their motivation is different from yours. An inability to recognize this has left many sincere, well-intentioned managers wondering why all their best efforts have failed.

What can managers do?

Motivation is an inner feeling, a drive that inspires and sustains action and commitment.

As a manager, you can't give people motivation the way you'd give them an assignment. But there is plenty you can do to create an environment where they are most likely to feel motivated to take actions that contribute to organizational goals. And while people have different needs and desires, the environment I'm talking about accommodates them all. In fact, it takes advantage of them all to create a high performing organization.

There's no mystery to what this environment looks like. It's one in which people believe their work is meaningful, have control over how they do it, have opportunities for growth and get feedback on their performance and recognition for their accomplishments. Oh yes, and a fair financial reward.

If you are a manager, creating such an environment is your number one task. This book offers advice based on practices that have worked in companies like yours, as well as the recommendations of the best thinkers in the field. You'll find out how to turn slackers into dedicated workers, coasters into contributors, lone wolfs into team players and superstars into loyalists, dedicated to your organization for the long term. They'll make these commitments not because they have to, but because they *want* to. That's what motivation really means.

But this book isn't only about motivating people who work for you. It's also about charging your own batteries and, if necessary, lighting a fire under a foot-dragging boss or lackadaisical colleagues, customers or suppliers. When you, your management and your peers are actively committed to the organization's vision and revved up by its challenges, you'll be more satisfied at work and you'll have a head start on creating a work unit where your employees feel the same.

Note

1   Spitzer, D.R. (1995) *Supermotivation*, AMACOM, New York, p.33.

Part I
Why Motivation
Matters

It doesn't take much motivation to do what your boss says, pick up your pay cheque and go home. But in a global, hi-tech world, organizations can't afford to follow the old paradigm of managers giving orders and workers complying with them. That's too big a waste of employees' knowledge, creativity and problem-solving smarts. And organizations need all the smarts they can tap.

Chapter 1 explores what motivates employees to devote their hearts, minds and extraordinary energy to their jobs, instead of simply putting in 'a fair day's work for a fair day's pay'.

Chapter 2 contends that any organization that wants to attract and retain the brightest and best workers had better know what turns them on. It examines the differences and similarities among the generations of people who make up today's workforce or are about to enter it.

Chapter 3 focuses on a basic and pragmatic reason for organizations to work harder at motivating the people who work for them. Low motivation costs an enterprise plenty in the form of absenteeism, sluggish performance and mistakes. That's too high a price to pay.

1

From Compliance to Commitment

In traditional organizations, management defines the jobs, assigns the work and determines how the tasks are to be done. Between management and employees, there is a contract – written or tacit – that says: 'You do as we say and we will reward you with an appropriate wage.' As long as both sides meet their contractual obligations, they are in compliance. The old union slogan of 'a fair day's work for a fair day's pay' describes the compact perfectly. It also suggests that 'a fair day's pay' is incentive enough to buy compliance.

> *Smart quotes*
>
> 'While economic rewards were pretty good for buying compliance, gaining commitment is a far different matter.'
>
> Kenneth W. Thomas, *Intrinsic Motivation at Work*[1]

Until a decade or so ago – still well within the memory of many working people – the contract had another clause: as long as you *continue* to fulfil our expectations, we will *continue* to reward you with an appropriate wage. When repeated downsizings, lay-offs, redundancies (you choose your term) shattered that clause, compliance began to erode.

But it wasn't just the demise of job security that undermined the capacity of compliance to ensure satisfactory performance. Perhaps even more important is the change in what organizations expect from their employees. Every enterprise faces global competition, challenging customer demands for quality and service, unprecedented requirements for technology that's obsolete as fast as it's installed, and the need to coax more out of a lean workforce. Confronting all that, companies are recognizing that the old paradigm – with management providing the knowledge and employees supplying the hands – doesn't work any more. In a knowledge-based economy, it's too big a waste of human capital to ignore the knowledge and potential for innovation of every employee.

So organizations expect employees to do more than follow orders these days. They expect them to solve problems, contribute original ideas, set challenging goals, figure out how to pursue them and participate in measuring their own performance and sometimes that of their boss and co-workers. And, oh yes, do all that while management is still hesitantly feeling its way into its own new, undefined role, and everybody's job is uncertain past the day after tomorrow.

This arrangement, characterized by change and flux, is very different from a contract for compliance. Compliance just doesn't cut it any more; without an imposed regimen, what is there to comply with? The new engagement expects employees to participate in determining the regimen, to modify it as circumstances change and to improve it continuously. That requires commitment, and winning that from employees is a whole different challenge for managers.

Winning employees' hearts and minds

Commitment is a function of the heart as well as the mind. One can rationally agree, 'In return for X reward, I'll work hard for eight or even ten hours a day.' But commitment is about caring, and nobody *rationally* decides to *care* for eight hours or ten or whatever it takes to get the job done.

Caring is a huge motivator. People care when the tasks are engaging, the outcomes important, the relationships satisfying and the whole experience increases their feeling of self-worth. They may even care enough to perform tasks that aren't engaging at all, rather are dull and mundane, if the other factors are strong enough.

Smart quotes

'Characteristics of organizations that enable either compliance or commitment

High control: compliance enabling	Low control: commitment enabling
Leaders rely on personal intelligence	Leaders commit to others' intelligence
Believe organizations can be fixed like machines	Believe organizations are run by human beings who have a free will, and cannot be "fixed"
Planning and direction are mandated	Action is driven by intention vs plans; consensus has priority over mandates
Little strategic information is shared	Everyone creates/shares strategic information
Have complex structures and many levels	Simple structures and few levels
Informal organization stores most of the energy	Informal organization is the formal organization
Values and structure inhibit sharing of ideas/information	Values/processes force sharing of ideas/information
Corporate solutions dominate and are mandated for all	Local solutions dominate and are not mandated for all'

William Becker, *How to OD ... And Live to Tell About It*[2]

Caring and commitment: another management fad?

You may be thinking, 'Yeah sure, last year it was pay for performance; this year let's get everyone to care; who knows what next year will bring.' But the truth is, while managers have stressed the compliance contract, employees have indicated for a long time that they longed for a different approach. As early as 1946, researchers in the United States asked a cross-section of employees to rank 10 'job reward factors' in terms of personal preference. The three top ranked factors were:

1   Full appreciation of work done.

2   Feeling of being in on things.

3   Sympathetic help with personal problems.

Professor Kenneth A. Kovach of George Mason University in Fairfax, Virginia gave the same list to 1000 employees in 1981 and 1995. By 1981, interesting work had bounced up to the top of the rankings and sympathetic help with personal problems had tumbled way down. In 1995, the top ranked items were:

1   Interesting work.

2   Full appreciation of work done.

3   Feeling of being in on things.

Both the original researchers and Professor Kovach also asked the employees' supervisors to rank the list *as they thought their employees had done*. The amazing thing is that managers have been pretty consistent in their ranking over the years – consistently very wrong. Here's what they've put on top:

1   Good wages.

2   Job security.

3   Promotion and growth in the organization.

Somebody hasn't been listening for at least 50 years!

Table 1.1 compares employee rankings in 1946 and 1995 to manager rankings for all ten items.

Table 1.1   What employees want – ranking of ten job reward factors.[3]

What managers said	Employees' ranking (1946)	Employees' ranking (1995)
1 Good wages	5	5
2 Job security	4	4
3 Promotion and growth in the organization	7	6
4 Good working conditions	9	8
5 Interesting work	6	1
6 Personal loyalty to employees	8	7
7 Tactful discipline	10	9
8 Full appreciation of work done	1	2
9 Sympathetic help with personal problems	3	10
10 Feeling of being in on things	2	3

Notice that the manager's rankings pretty much match the concept of a compliance contract. The employees' lists look a lot more like the basis for commitment. Or, described another way, the managers are talking about extrinsic rewards and the employees are more focused on intrinsic rewards.

Intrinsic and extrinsic motivation

When the purists insist we can't motivate anyone else, that we can only motivate ourselves, they are talking about *intrinsic* motivation, the kind that comes from within. If I get enjoyment out of putting my ideas into words and seeing them appear on the computer screen, that is intrinsic motivation for the task of writing. If I get satisfaction from helping others solve a work problem, that motivates me to consult with clients and lead management seminars. If I get a kick out of tinkering with the toolbar buttons and discovering new ways to create graphics, that sees me through the frustration of learning yet another upgraded version of PowerPoint.

Mostly we think of intrinsic motivation as liking to do the work. That's why we seek out jobs in fields we enjoy. But it isn't all that direct. There are workers who go to work every day and perform quite satisfactorily because they enjoy socializing with their co-workers. For some jobs that would be a distraction, but for others, such as many assembly line jobs, enjoying one's co-workers can be motivation enough. Another employee may not be too excited by the specific task he's assigned on a project, but the opportunity to work closely with the others on the team might be enough intrinsic motivation to keep him contributing with enthusiasm.

Sometimes it's not the task that lures us but the outcome. Writing, for example, is not always enjoyable. In fact, much of the time, it's gruelling, frustrating work. But it is always a thrill to hold a book in my hand with my name on it. To find out that a professor assigns one of my books to his students or a seminar leader makes one required reading for her participants – those things give my self-worth a tremendous boost. So I go on writing in anticipation of the reward of good feelings to come.

Most of the time when we are working for delayed gratification, we're propelled by extrinsic motivation, something we're expecting to get from outside ourselves. Usually, that means financial rewards or similar incentives, on the one hand, and the threat of punishment if we screw up on the other. It's not the fun of the task or the pleasure in the outcome that spurs us on. What we want is the reward and the work is simply what we have to do to get it – or to avoid the punishment.

The contract for compliance was mostly about extrinsic motivation, and the era of commitment depends upon intrinsic motivation. But, of course, it would be naive to assume that it is ever either/or. There are assembly line workers who make their work interesting by challenging themselves and each other to work faster and more ac-curately, getting a thrill out of beating their own and their co-workers' records. And however interesting the work and meaningful the outcome, you'll be hard pressed to find and keep employees if you don't pay them a living wage – or perhaps an exceptional one if your competi-tor has deeper pockets, and people can do similar work for more money elsewhere.

So it takes a combination of motivators to spur people into high perform-ance. Some, like financial incentives and company honours, are bestowed

A funny thing about motivation: it can strike when you least expect it. Kenneth W. Thomas was the co-author of a popular conflict-style self-assessment instrument[5] and had just been promoted to full professor at the University of Pittsburgh. It looked like a high point in his career, but Thomas was feeling a little burned out so he jumped at an opportunity to spend six months on the faculty of the Naval Postgraduate School in Monterey, California. He had visions of sitting on the sand, staring out over the Pacific, and contemplating the meaning of life.

Smart quotes

'Extrinsic motivation is caused by positive and nega-tive incentives. Carrots and sticks. These are most effec-tive when people are in need or afraid. Well-fed people do not jump for carrots, and self-confident people do not allow bosses to beat them.'

Michael Maccoby, *Why Work?*[4]

SMART PEOPLE
TO HAVE ON
YOUR SIDE:

KENNETH W.
THOMAS

But one thought led to another, and pretty soon he didn't have much time for beachcombing any more. Instead, he threw himself into research on what it was that energized people.

'When I was teaching motivation in those days,' he recalls, 'it was mostly expectancy theory – rational, delayed gratification. It became clear to me that a lot of the old models were almost irrelevant in explaining what energizes you.'[6] There was nothing in expectancy theory about the rewards of the work experience itself.

From his research with Betty Velthouse[7] he compiled a list of motivating factors and boiled them down to four: sense of choice, sense of competence, sense of meaningfulness and sense of progress. 'Then I began to realize where they had come from,' Thomas explains. 'Two came from activities and two from purposes.' It is motivating for workers to have a choice of activities – to decide for themselves how they are going to do their work – and to increase their competency as they perform tasks. It is also motivating for people to know that they are working toward a meaningful purpose and to experience progress as they achieve positive results.'

Thomas says he was particularly influenced by psychologist Edward L. Deci, who has conducted numerous experiments into intrinsic motivation, and by the work of J. Richard Hackman and Greg R. Oldham in job redesign.[8] Through Deci's work, he expanded his understanding of the intrinsic rewards that come from task activities. Hackman and Oldham focused Thomas's attention on outcomes, roughly comparable to what he calls purpose. But Thomas thinks concentrating on either task activities or outcomes leaves something out. 'So basically, I took from Hackman and Oldham and combined that with Deci, and it seems to work very well,' he asserts.

Thomas (with co-author Walter G. Tymon) published a model of Four Intrinsic Rewards:[9]

	OPPORTUNITY Rewards	ACCOMPLISHMENT Rewards
From task ACTIVITIES	Sense of choice	Sense of competence
From task PURPOSE	Sense of meaningfulness	Sense of progress

In his book, *Intrinsic Motivation at Work*[10], Thomas defines these four intrinsic rewards. For the first two, he notes, the reward is in the opportunity; for the second two it is in the accomplishment.

- *Meaningfulness*: pursuing a task 'worth your time and energy', whose 'purpose matters in the larger scheme of things'.
- *Choice*: being able to 'select activities that make sense to you and perform them in ways that seem appropriate'.
- *Competence*: 'skilfully performing task activities you have chosen'.
- *Progress*: 'achieving the task purpose' as well as moving forward toward accomplishing a goal.

Thomas stresses the importance of having a vocabulary that defines intrinsic motivation and getting people to talk about it. 'It's important diagnostically,' he asserts. 'Deming used to talk about joy in work. As a phrase, that doesn't help you. Saying "Wow, I'm not having much joy in work," doesn't solve anything. But if you know joy is composed of meaningfulness, choice, competence, and progress, then you can assess what's gone wrong and which building blocks to go after.'

Kenneth Thomas knows first hand about going after building blocks. While his first six-month stint at the Naval Postgraduate School ended as scheduled, he knew he'd found a key there to his own motivation and eventually returned to take up a permanent position as professor of management.

by others. As a manager, you have at least some control over these. Others do come from within, but that doesn't let you off the hook, because there are plenty of things you can do to make it more likely that your employees will discover these motivators within themselves.

Even when you know what resources you have for energizing your employees, it is still difficult is to figure out which motivators will be more effective with specific people at particular times. Theorists have been researching this issue and proposing solutions for years. Probably the best known in the business world are Abraham Maslow and Frederick Herzberg. Their models have been around for many years, and you could say that most newer theories are outgrowths of these two.

The grand masters of motivational theory[11]

Maslow's hierarchy of needs[12]

Abraham Maslow has probably influenced the teaching of management more than any other motivational theorist. He identified five basic needs that, he maintained, we all strive to fulfil in our work as well as in the other aspects of our lives. Then he arranged the five needs into a hierarchy, the lowest being purely physical and the highest transcendent (see Fig. 1.1).

People are primarily motivated by their lowest unmet need, Maslow maintained, and here's where most later theorists disagree with Maslow, pointing out numerous examples where people are obviously operating off a higher need while a lower one is still unmet. The starving artist seeking self-actualization is a favourite example. Even Maslow noted that the sequence was not immutable. And yet, there are also plenty of illustrations to support his hierarchical model:

Self-actualization: becoming all one is capable of being.

Esteem: self-respect, and respect from others.

Belongingness and love.

Safety: security, stability, structure.

Physiological: food, drink, sex. Freedom from pain.

Fig. 1.1   Maslow's hierarchy of needs.

- If you are starving, you may risk your life (ignoring safety needs) to get food.

- After you take a job to satisfy your security needs, you want to make friends (belonging and love) with your co-workers. Then pretty soon you expect the company to demonstrate its esteem for you by giving you a promotion.

- But if your office pals throw a party to celebrate your promotion, surrounding you with affection and admiration, and in the middle of it you learn your house is on fire, your belonging and esteem needs will take a back seat to safety as you rush home.

For the most part, Maslow believed, humans proceed up the ladder of needs in order, propelled toward the next need as each is satisfied – to the point of satisfying the esteem need. Here, he maintained, many people are content to stop. Those that go on, the self-actualizers, are motivated not by a deficiency but by a desire to grow. They exhibit greater creativity, more profound sense of humour, greater appreciation of a variety of experiences, and greater acceptance of themselves, others and nature. (On the other hand, he described some self-actualizers as unsympathetic, egocentric, discourteous, antisocial and guilt-prone.)

Herzberg's Motivation–Hygiene Theory[13]

While the proponents of each point out significant differences between Maslow's Hierarchy and Frederick Herzberg's Motivation–Hygiene Theory, for most managers moving from Maslow to Herzberg isn't much of a leap. They both describe the same kinds of needs. Instead of arranging these needs in a hierarchy, however, Herzberg divided them all into two categories, labelled hygiene factors and motivators (see Table 1.2). The hygiene factors make up the job context; the motivators are all related to the job content.

You can see that most of the hygiene factors correspond with the lower levels of Maslow's hierarchy and the motivators match the higher levels. But Herzberg didn't see the factors as a progression, rather as two sets, both operative at the same time.

Think of an employee as sitting on one side of a balance scale. To keep balanced, the employee requires the hygiene factors on the other side. Remove them and the worker gets bounced around tumultuously. But all these do is keep the balance, Herzberg insisted; they don't motivate the worker to greater productivity and creativity. Now, if you weight that side of the scale with the motivators, the worker soars to new heights.

Table 1.2 Hygiene factors and motivators.

Hygiene factors	Motivators
Company policy and administration	Achievement
Supervision	Recognition
Relationship with supervisor	Work itself – job content
Work conditions	Responsibility
Salary	Advancement
Relationship with peers	Growth
Personal life	
Relationship with subordinates	
Status	
Security	

Put another way, if you withhold the hygiene factors, you can depend upon having a dissatisfied worker. Providing them, however, won't guarantee you a satisfied, energized one. Satisfaction on the job comes from the fulfilment of the motivators.

One of the characteristics of the current generation of workers is that they take the hygiene factors for granted. They grew up in an environment where all these factors were satisfied. In fact, finding some of them lacking in the workplace can be a disorienting jolt. But their primary mode of operating is a constant pursuit of Herzberg's motivators. Maslow suggested that each need except self-actualization has a satiation point, but there is nothing in Herzberg's theory to predict that at some point an individual will say, 'OK, that's enough. I don't need any more.'

Happily, Herzberg's theory is prescriptive as well as descriptive. The way to improve workers' motivation, he maintained, is by enriching their jobs. You can do that, he said, by removing controls, increasing a worker's account-ability, giving a person a complete natural unit of work rather than discrete tasks, introducing new and more difficult tasks, and assigning specialized tasks that allow a person to become an expert.

Managers have been studying Maslow and Herzberg since the 1950s and '60s, and still, until recently, companies relied primarily on buying compliance from their workers. It's taken a new world economic climate, technology that has turned the management–employee compact topsy-turvy, and a generation of workers with new demands to awaken most organizations to the realization that you can't buy commitment, but you can earn it by creating a new kind of work environment.

The smartest things in this chapter

- The traditional management/employee compliance contract doesn't work in an environment where employees are expected to think for themselves, contribute ideas and solve problems.

- Intrinsic motivation comes from pleasure provided by the work itself.

- Extrinsic motivation comes from the pleasure of a reward.

- Abraham Maslow, one of the most influential motivational theorists, defined a hierarchy of human needs, and maintained that each of us is motivated by our lowest unmet need.

- Frederick Herzberg, another prominent theorist, recognized two kinds of needs: hygiene factors that come from job context and motivators that are related to job content.

Notes

1 Thomas, K.W. (2000) *Intrinsic Motivation at Work*. Berrett-Koehler, San Francisco, p.5.

2 Becker, W. (2002) *How to OD ... and Live to Tell About It*. Xlibris, Philadelphia, PA, p.27.

3 Results based on 'Employee Motivation: Addressing a Crucial Factor in Your Organization's Performance', a report prepared by Kenneth A. Kovach of George Mason University.

4 Maccoby, M. (1995) *Why Work?* (2e). Miles River Press, Alexandria, Virginia, p.7.

5 Thomas, K.W. & R.H. Kilmann (1974) *Thomas–Kilmann Conflict Mode Instrument*. CPP, Inc., Palto Alto, CA.

6 Unless otherwise noted, the quotes here are from an interview with Thomas in spring 2002.

7 Thomas, K.W. & B.A. Velthouse 'Cognitive elements of empowerment: An interpretive model of intrinsic task motivation' in *Academy of Management Review*, 15, no. 4 (1990), pp.666–81.

8 See Deci, E.L. & R. Flaste *Why We Do What We Do* (1996 reprint edition). Penguin, New York, and Hackman, J.R. & G.R. Oldham (1980) *Work Redesign*. Addison-Wesley, Boston.

9 From K.W. Thomas and W.G. Tymon (1996) *Empowerment Inventory*. CPP, Inc., Palo Alto, CA.

10 Thomas, K.W. (2000) *Intrinsic Motivation at Work*. Berrett-Koehler, San Francisco, p.44.

11 These summaries of the theories of Maslow and Herzberg are based upon material written by the author for the American Management Association's seminar, Motivating Others. This material is © 1990 American Management Association and is used with permission.

12 Maslow, A.H. (1954) *Motivation and Personality*. Harper & Row, New York.

13 Herzberg, F. 'One more time: How do you motivate employees?' in *Harvard Business Review*, September–October 1987, p.109 (reprinted as an HBR Classic from the January–February 1968 issue).

2

Attracting and Retaining Today's Best Talent

Most new employees start out eager, willing and full of energy. As a manager, you'd have the motivation issue licked if you could just count on their staying that way and staying with you. It helps if you know before you ever hire them:

- what turns them on – and if your organization can provide whatever that is;

- whether their values and expectations match yours; and

- if the work they'd love to do is work your organization needs to have done.

Companies that confirm those matches during their hiring processes have higher performing employees and better retention records. One such enterprise is Hill's Pet Nutrition, a favourite example of Jon Katzenbach, author of *Peak Performance*. As Katzenbach explains, it takes six months to get hired into a Hill's factory. During that time, potential employees visit various parts of the plant and spend time there with workers in different settings. By the end of the process, both recruit and company know whether there is a good fit between them. Incidentally, this gruelling but effective recruiting process was the brainchild, not of management nor of human resources, but of the workers themselves.[1] In his book, Katzenbach notes that among technicians at the company's prototype plant, the turnover rate is only 5 per cent annually, compared to 17 per cent per month for some manufacturers in the same area.[2]

But even before you begin the hiring process, you can learn a lot about your potential employees from the wealth of studies that have been done on what motivates today's workforce.

Insights and stereotypes

If you judge potential hirees by newspaper headlines, they fall into two widely divergent categories: impatient baby moguls on the one hand and, on the other, a poorly educated, poor prepared underclass weaned on welfare, not work. Stereotypical as these labels are, in all probability you've met examples of both.

Until the bursting of the dot-com bubble and the subsequent economic slowdown, you would have thought every 21-year-old expected to be rich before reaching 30. Indeed, the business press was full of articles with titles like 'How to Manage a Millionaire', giving advice for coaxing stock-wealthy employees to do the mundane work necessary in even the most innovative companies. Fewer companies have that exact problem any more, but they are still learning to cope with young, techno-savvy upstarts who demand fascinating opportunities and control over their own jobs, unfettered by bureaucracy.

Then there is the other end of the spectrum. Across the United States, public schools struggle with falling academic test scores and are criticized for sending woefully unprepared young people out into the world. In the UK, the effort goes on to break a generations-long pattern of life on the dole. In both countries, critics describe legions of should-be workers with neither the skills nor the will to become productive members of the workforce. Confronted with a talent pool like this, managers of workers in low-level service jobs have problems hiring, motivating and retaining workers.

'We've got to do more than just teach our children skills and knowledge. That's one part of education, and it's an important part, no question about it … Our children must learn to make a living, but even more, they must learn how to live.'

President George W. Bush[3]

 SMART VOICES

'We must not only lift people out of poverty. We must transform their horizons, aspirations and hopes as well – through helping people get the skills they need for better jobs.'

Prime Minister Tony Blair[4]

SMART VOICES

But those are the stereotypes, and like all stereotypes they accurately describe only a visible few. The great majority of people in today's workforce

SMART PEOPLE
TO HAVE ON
YOUR SIDE:

MICHAEL
MACCOBY

An anthropologist and psychoanalyst as well as a management consultant, Michael Maccoby brought a range of perspectives to the topic of motivation when he wrote the book entitled with a question, *Why Work?*

A short answer to the title question is, 'In the final analysis, most people need to work, not only for material rewards, but because they want to exercise their abilities and to feel valuable to themselves and to others.'[5]

That poses another question: What makes people feel valuable? Maccoby identified eight 'value drives' in the workplace: security, relatedness, pleasure, information, mastery, play, dignity and meaning. Jobs and workplaces that provide these things motivate people to perform their best and to commit themselves to the organization.

But we're not all looking for all of these in equal doses. For each of us some are more important than others. Dominant value drives help to differentiate five different character types Maccoby describes: expert, helper, defender, innovator and self-developer.

The first four show up strongly among the Baby Boomers and the generation that preceded them. The fifth type, self-developers, are the poster children of Generation X.

As a group to be reckoned with, self-developers appeared on the scene in the 1980s and, to a large degree, changed the nature of the workforce in the 1990s – an era they seemed particularly suited for. Brought up during a time of change, they adapt easily to it. They care less about job security than about learning new skills, gaining new experiences and staying marketable. They network well and work well in teams, and yet they are fiercely independent.

Based on *Why Work?*, the table that follows shows how self-developers compare to Maccoby's other four types in terms of defining characteristics, the values that drive them and the conditions that motivate them.

Character type	Defining characteristics	Dominant value drives	Motivators
Self-developers	Want to learn, willing to take risks. Dislike bureaucracy. More impressed by competence than status or authority. Demand a balance between work and personal life.	Mastery, information, play, pleasure	Opportunities to learn, develop competence, maintain employability
Innovators	Want to change the world, realize their visions. May accomplish breakthrough inventions or new kinds of organizations.	Play, mastery	Opportunities to create
Experts	Want to demonstrate their knowledge, master challenges and gain recognition. Want status, control and respect. Predominate in top management.	Mastery	Challenge, recognition
Helpers	Care for people. Want to feel needed, respected and heard. Sociable. Often found in helping professions and service sector.	Relatedness	Opportunities to help
Defenders	Want to establish justice, protect people from wrongdoing. May distrust outsiders, use threats and rewards to control others.	Dignity, mastery	Challenges to right wrongs

Michael Maccoby is the author of *The Gamesman* (1977), *The Leader* (1981) and *Sweden at the Edge, Lessons for American and Swedish Managers* (1995), as well as *Why Work?* With psychoanalyst Eric Fromm, he also wrote *Social Character in a Mexican Village* (1970). He has taught at Harvard, University of Chicago, Cornell University, University of California, l'Institut d'Etudes Politiques de Paris and the Washington School of Psychiatry, where he is emeritus professor. He is president of The Maccoby Group in Washington, DC and director of the Project on Technology, Work and Character, a not-for-profit research organization.

are neither self-centred hot-doggers nor hopelessly work-aversive. But they do have some generational distinctions. Recognizing these can help you, as a manager, perform a mental 'fit' test when you are recruiting new employees. It can also give you insight to provide the support your employees need if they are to be motivated and committed members of your organization, dedicated to doing their part to meet organizational goals.

Boomers and the alphabet generations

They are not called Baby Boomers for nothing: the birth rate boomed after World War II until the early '60s. The result was a generation that would be notable just for its size if nothing else. They are still the largest group in the workforce and will remain so for several years since the oldest among them are just beginning to contemplate retirement. But they have a lot more than just numbers to define themselves by. Boomers strive to 'make it' and want the world to know when they arrive. They wear their status symbols – be they corporate titles or designer clothes – with pride.

Boomers' parents worked hard to give their families a good life, and the lesson was not lost on their offspring, who turned long, hard work hours and the pursuit of professional success into a fine art. They willingly sacrificed free time and personal life to gain another rung on the ladder. With career paths ahead of them, they had good reason to be loyal employees. Although they chafe at the betrayal of the compliance contract by downsizing companies, many Boomers still extol loyalty as a worthy value and decry the lack of it among their successors – that generation with the ignominious label, Generation X.

Nobody quite knew what to make of Gen Xers when they burst upon the work scene in the early '80s. No sacrifice for them – they wanted everything now: exciting assignments, good pay, fun at work and lots of free time to pursue other activities. They weren't particularly impressed by titles or status, so if they didn't get what they wanted, they were quite likely to toss aside the whole corporate thing and become yoga instructors. It all sounded pretty irrational to the Boomers, who viewed them as unreasonable and lazy.

But in the '90s, Gen Xers came into their own. Maybe they weren't very loyal, but they weren't devastated by company downsizings either. They cared more about job content than job title, so they fitted well into flattened organizations with collapsed promotional ladders. They shone in smaller, entrepreneurial organizations and thrived in the fast-changing technological world.

Smart quotes

'They don't buy into hierarchy for the sake of hierarchy. They don't respond to authority by virtue of a title. Which is exactly how the boomers responded when they first entered the workplace. Now they have to practice what they preached when they were younger.'

Neil Stroul, organizational psychologist[6]

The work–family issue

Boomers are famous for their willingness to put in long hours at work and to uproot themselves and their families and move off to their next assignment on the other side of the country or world, at their companies' call. Gen Xers, many of them growing up in those families, often with two parents working the same difficult schedules, are more inclined to say, 'I don't think so. I want a life outside work.' Although these two attitudes are most often described as a generational difference, there is also an era difference. In fact, starting in the '90s, workers of all generations began to protest this disruption to their personal lives.

Cheryl Lazzaro, a managing director in human resources in a hi-tech organization, watched sadly as long work hours drove away a high-potential employee, but she and her firm's management learned their lesson and lured him back. 'He had been with us at least seven years,' she recalls. 'He grew up on the technical side, then went into technical management. He had been recognized and rewarded financially by the organization. But he worked ungodly hours, which was not to the benefit of his personal life and his family. We had once talked about his taking a sabbatical away from this company as a development opportunity.'[7]

Before that happened he got an offer from another company for a new job with fewer hours and more money. He went there for a little over a year. But his former employer didn't forget him. During that time, says Lazzaro, 'There was a lot of dialogue going on, a great desire on our part to bring him back.' Both sides learned some things. Forced to get along without him, his former manager learned the work could get done without leaning so hard on this one person. In moving to the new job, the former employee learned to take more responsibility for managing his own work–life balance.

Finally, he came back. When he did, he told Lazzaro, 'It was sort of like that sabbatical you talked about. I went outside, learned some things and learned a lot about myself. On this new assignment I have more ability to manage my own expectations.'

Boomers and Xers through a Herzberg lens

Hank Karp explored the generational chasm for the book, *Bridging the Boomer Xer Gap*.[8] Karp heads up a consulting organization called Personal Growth Systems in Chesapeake, Virginia, and is an associate professor on the faculty of management at Hampton University. In an interview, he shared his insights as he fielded a barrage of questions: What makes Gen Xers tick? What turns them on and revs them up? How are they different from Baby Boomers?

'In terms of what motivates them,' he responded, 'nothing different.' Before the shock of that reply set in, he went on to explain what he meant by that, and why it was only a part of the story.

Karp, who studied for his doctorate under Frederick Herzberg at Case Western University, looks at motivation through the Herzberg framework. The word motivators is reserved strictly for factors like achievement, recognition for achievement, work content, responsibility, advancement and growth. Those things, Karp says, will motivate both Baby Boomers and Gen Xers to stellar performance.

Things like salary, work conditions, relationships with others on the job and even status are what Herzberg calls hygiene. Regarding those things, Karp asserts, Gen Xers are very different from their predecessors. Boomers put a lot more value on them than do Gen Xers, to the extent that, in a workplace with positive hygiene factors, Boomers will grit their teeth and tolerate the absence of true motivators. Gen Xers won't.

For example, says Karp:

- If you give them repetitive work, Xers will quit and leave; Boomers will quit and stay.

- When the work is not engaging, Xers will be vocal and Boomers will put up with it without complaining.

- Boomers dream of working 30 years, getting a gold watch and retiring to Arizona; Xers don't expect to stay with one company.

- A big payoff for Boomers is the pension plan; for Xers, it's working conditions that offer freedom, resources and opportunities.

- Boomers expect to pay their dues; Xers want responsibility right away.

- Layoffs are an incredibly big deal for Boomers; for Xers they're no big deal.

- Boomers want overtime; Xers want compensatory time.

- Boomers will put in 60-hour work weeks because it makes them look good in the company; Xers will do it if 'the project demands it'.

- Boomers are into organizational identity, Xers into individual identity.

'Loyalty,' says Karp, 'is a big differentiating factor. For Boomers, loyalty is a value. It's not part of the Xers' value system. Treat them well, with respect, and let them contribute, and they'll be loyal. But treat them like a number, a tool for productivity, and they'll be gone.'

One thing about their research surprised Karp and his co-authors. For all their individuality, Xers are very team-oriented, they discovered. But their concept of a team is different from that of Boomers. The traditional team building model, Karp explains, is based on similarities and commonalities. The Xers' approach values people's differences. 'The commonality is in the objective,' says Karp, 'not in who they are or their values.'

Karp points out that this is more of a Gestalt approach. Teaming the Gen X way is not about trying to change people to be more alike, but in getting them focused on the same objectives.

A contrarian view of generational differences

Just when you think you've got the generation gap all figured out, along comes evidence that it's not that clear cut. When Professor Kovach, who ran the 1995 survey described in Chapter 1, broke his outcomes down by age group, he found some results that are not quite in sync with the prevailing view of Gen Xers described above. Among under-age-30 respondents, the top three preferred rewards were:

1   Good wages.

2   Job security.

3   Promotion and growth in the organization.

Interesting work and full appreciation of work done did not hit the list until number 4 and 5. Kovach looked to Maslow for an explanation, suggesting that young people were still struggling to meet their lower needs on Maslow's hierarchy.

Perhaps the best lesson to be learned is that while general group characteristics are useful, it's a big risk to assume they are a perfect fit with any individual.

Then came Generation Y

First off, here's a good thing to remember. If you want to establish rapport with Gen Yers, don't call them that. They think it's demeaning to be labelled with a letter whose only significance is that it follows X. (Come to think of it, Gen Xers aren't thrilled with their tagline either. After all, they got stuck with it just because nobody knew what else to call them.) But because these are the most common labels, this book will go on referring to them as X and Y.

In their book, *Generations at Work*, Ron Zemke, Claire Raines and Bob Filipczak called this group, born after 1980, 'Nexters'. That's better than Gen Y, perhaps, since it suggests that they are the next big thing. Which they are. In the United States, they represent a huge population surge, and the oldest among them are just getting out of college and entering the adult workforce.

SMART VOICES

'This is a very pragmatic group. At 18 years old, they have five-year plans. They are already looking at how they will be balancing their work/family commitments.'

Deanna Tillisch, who directed a 1998 survey of college freshman for Northwestern Mutual Life Insurance Company.[9]

Call them what you will, many researchers are calling them traditional, committed, ambitious and empowered. They want steady jobs, but they're also thinking about having families and expect to balance the two. Gen Xers hit the workforce well schooled in technology, but these youngsters were born into it; it's practically a part of their DNA.

Two researchers, Kathy Pennell and Fred Martels, studied 352 employed teenagers in St Louis, Missouri and Rochester, NY. The teens told Pennell and Martels that pride in their job and respect for what they do are more important to them than money. What else is important? For their book, *The Teenage Worker*, Pennell and Martel compiled a list of factors that affect teenage worker retention. Among the top five, money ranks fourth, as follows:

Smart quotes

Tips for motivating the different generations:

Boomers: 'give them lots of public recognition.'

Xers: 'give them lots of projects. Let them take control of prioritizing and juggling.'

Nexters: 'learn about their personal goals. Show how they mesh with the company's.'

Ron Zemke, Claire Raines and Bob Filipczak[10]

1   Being treated with respect.

2   Being treated fairly.

3   Flexible scheduling.

4   Money/pay.

5   Fun place to work.[11]

And don't forget the veterans

Before the Baby Boomers came along, the pundits hadn't started naming the generations. Now some people are calling the pre-Boomers 'Veterans'. But by any name, they haven't all moved to Florida and Spain yet. Plenty of them are still pulling their weight at all levels and all functions in the workforce.

Probably the key to motivating them is to remember that their brains haven't atrophied, nor has their desire to learn and innovate. Younger managers have a tendency to assume anyone looking at either side of 60 is waiting out retirement. Far from it. The best way to turn them on is to offer them new challenges. Oh sure, there are some curmudgeons who will insist they've tried it all before and none of it works – no matter what 'it' is – but give them a chance to get their feet wet and those very curmudgeons will become each new project's strongest advocate.

Retaining top talent – from all generations

Motivated to work and *motivated to work for your organization* may not be synonymous. When they're not, you lose your best performers. One organization with a concentrated effort to keep that from happening is the Securities Industry Automation Corporation (SIAC), which provides key systems support to the New York and American Stock Exchanges, Depository Trust and Clearing Corporation and the securities industry nationwide.

A part of that effort is conducting exit interviews, not only when some-one leaves, but also one year later, because people are more willing to talk frankly then. Joseph Meilan, senior vice president of Human Resources, Corporate Communications and Legal Services, says what motivates peo-ple to leave are 'money and management, not necessarily in that order'.[12]

'Usually the manager is not motivating them, not showing attention to their career and growth, not recognizing them for their accomplishments. It's not all about money. If you want to keep good people,' says Meilan, 'you have to have a strong, top-down philosophical emphasis, an environment that says you are paying attention to people, they are important as individuals and important as part of teams. And you also need a compensation system that says the same, with incentives tied to how people perform.'

For members of any generation, that philosophy works at SIAC for motivating people to perform their best and for keeping them around when they do.

The smartest things in this chapter

- To hire and keep a top-performing Baby Boomer, emphasize status and recognition.

- To hang on to Gen Xers, give them control over their own work and new challenges to address.

- You can motivate ambitious, young Gen Yers by linking your company's opportunities to the goals in their long-term career plans.

- Pre-Boomers are still turned on by new challenges and opportunities to learn.

Notes

1 Described by Jon Katzenbach in an interview in spring 2002.

2 Katzenbach, J. (2000) *Peak Performance*. Harvard Business School Press, Boston, page 94.

3 Speaking at the White House Conference on Character and Community, 19 June 2002.

4 From a speech on welfare reform, June 10, 2002.

5 Maccoby, M. (1995) *Why Work?* (2e). Miles River Press, Alexandria, VA, p.253.

6 Quoted in 'Warring Generations Are Much the Same' by Tracy Wenzel Conner in *Northwest Florida Daily News*, 8 November 1998, p.1F.

7 From an interview in summer 2002.

8 Karp, H., C. Fuller & D. Sirias (2002) *Bridging the Boomer Xer Gap*. Davies-Black, Palo Alto, CA.

9 Quoted in *Business Week Online*, 15 February 1998.

10 Quoted from www.amanet.org, based on the book Zemke, R., C. Raines & B. Filipczak (1999) *Generations at Work*. AMACOM, New York.

11 Martels, F. & K. Pennell (2000) *The Teenage Worker*. Teenage Workforce Solutions, St. Louis, MO.

12 From an interview in summer 2002.

3

The Performance Connection: The Cost of Low Motivation

When psychologists talk about motivation, they're talking about internal drives, subconscious needs and personal fulfilment.

But when managers talk about motivation, they're talking about something much more visible: *performance*. When they say they want motivated employees, they mean employees who fulfil job expectations and pitch in to help others or work extra hours when needed. They expect employees who want to get ahead in the company to show some extra gumption by learning new skills and taking on additional tasks. In practical terms, that's motivation at work.

A lot of managers will grumble that motivation at work is something they just don't see enough of. 'I have never found

> Smart things
> to say about motivation
>
> In the workplace, lack of motivation isn't about psychology. It's about things like absenteeism, low productivity and repeated mistakes.

it so hard to motivate people,' lamented a veteran manager in an insurance claims office. 'They have a good incentive pay system, but they do only what they need to, and that with resentment.' He went on to tell of a work unit plagued by absenteeism, low productivity and lack of accountability for accuracy.

It wasn't supposed to be that way. In fact, the company had restructured its claims offices with the expectation of improved productivity and customer satisfaction. It had implemented a new pay-for-performance programme, and automated and reorganized to make it easier for the claims processors to resolve more claims faster. The employees, the manager lamented, handled the companies' more complicated claims and were paid according to the number of claims they processed. It was a job that used to involve concern for the insured, on which the company prided itself, along with judgement and decision making. In the old days, if a claim was really complicated, the employee might discuss it with colleagues, and they'd work out a solution together. But now, all the employees did was feed the claim information into the computer, and the system did all the judging. Even the customer contact part was gone; in the name of efficiency, any questions for (or complaints from) the insureds were fielded by a dedicated customer service unit.

Ironically, while the customer service representatives relieved them of dealing with upset, often bereaved, customers, the stress level of the claims processors seemed higher, not lower. And while the restructuring had increased their potential for pay increases, few of them consistently took advantage of it. Instead they took all their sick days and slipped out early whenever possible. They bumped an excessive number of claims up to a dedicated technical support staff. They didn't quit and go elsewhere; mostly they were working moms with kids in school, and there weren't many jobs that offered comparable pay and flexibility in terms of work hours. But, in a way, they did quit; they just didn't leave.

When managers complain that their employees lack motivation, they're talking about tangible workplace problems like absenteeism, task avoidance, and mistakes no one bothers to correct. 'It's not the money; we pay them decently,' a frustrated manager will quickly assert, as if that relieves the organization of culpability. If money doesn't drive performance, an 'enlightened' company might send the offending employees off to training. When that doesn't work, the manager resorts to punishment, but even that has only a temporary impact. So, stuck for an answer to the problem, the manager is likely to conclude that employees these days don't want to work. They just aren't motivated.

That's a handy diagnosis. It lets the manager off the hook and puts the blame squarely on the workers. It's their fault; they aren't motivated the way 'we' used to be. But even if it is true, it doesn't lessen the need to solve the problem because, for employers, the cost of poor motivation is too high a price to pay. Poor motivation is a label that encompasses a range of expensive behaviours and attitudes, from absenteeism to careless mistakes.

KILLER QUESTIONS

Why aren't *they* motivated the way *we* used to be?

Deciding between going to work or staying in bed

Employees stay away when they get more gratification from being elsewhere than from coming to work. If sleeping in or going shopping offers more rewards than typing and filing or any other job tasks, then some people are going to exploit every opportunity to indulge in the more satisfying behaviour.

Take the example of the elusive administrative assistant to the director of a corporate training department. He was a fast and accurate typist, charming in his contact with his boss's peers, interested in the department's programmes, and a lot of fun to be around. He was all those things, that is, when he went to work. But he also used up all his vacation, his personal days and his sick days on no-shows, calling in at the last minute with the flimsiest of reasons. Confronted with having his pay docked for each absence, he finally improved his attendance slightly, but he also got more creative with his excuses. And, of course, as the year turned over, he had a whole new set of legitimate days off to take advantage of.

Eventually he left on his own accord for a higher paying job at the post office. Months later, when he returned for a visit he told the trainers in the department that yes, he liked the post office fine; the pay was good. But, he added, the work was boring and he missed his conversations with the corporate trainers about their programmes.

In truth, the trainers had pegged him as bright but lazy. They'd never thought of encouraging him to get more involved in their jobs. And their boss didn't either, since it was a challenge just to get this assistant into the office often enough to finish the clerical work. Nobody tried luring him out of bed in the morning with intellectual challenge and holding him accountable for stepping up to it.

Punishment is almost useless against chronic absenteeism in large companies because many of them have sick-leave policies that provide plenty of opportunities for abuse by healthy workers who are willing to fake aches, pains, colds and stomach ailments. Employees like that can wreak havoc on work schedules without crossing over into actionable territory for major discipline. The only really effective defence against absenteeism is to make coming to work more desirable than staying away. To be that, work has to boost the individual's self-worth, sense

Smart quotes

'Attempts to apply stricter discipline have been largely ineffectual ... An alternative approach begins not with blame and control, but with asking why people are behaving irresponsibly in the first place ... It then addresses the factors that can lead people to behave more responsibly.'

Edward L. Deci, *Why We Do What We Do*[1]

of control and pride in a way that staying in bed, playing golf or hanging out with friends can't measure up to.

The fine art of being absent on the job

There's more than one kind of absenteeism. Just as damaging, and perhaps more insidious, is the version that is masked by the presence of warm bodies in the workplace. But for all they contribute, these people might as well be home. When you need them, they are on the phone, down the hall, engaged in some mysterious other project, or just on their way to lunch.

It's hard to pinpoint their shortcomings because absent-on-the-job employees are often masters at obfuscation. In a team, they'll find a way to look convincingly busy while everyone else does the work. Ask them for sugges-

---

Q: What do I do with a person who just doesn't *want* to work?

A: Michael Maccoby, author of *Why Work?*, responds, 'The real question is whether the manager has done everything necessary to motivate.'[2] He offers the 4 Rs of motivation:

- *Responsibilities.* Matching skills and values to job responsibilities. This includes, for example, putting people with helper values into jobs where they are helping others.
- *Rewards.* Do people feel they are recognized, rewarded and appreciated – and given tough feedback when they need a push?
- *Relationships.* Are they treated with respect in their interactions with their boss, customers and co-workers?
- *Reasons.* People often feel what they do is meaningless, Maccoby has found, because their managers don't tell them why when they assign a task or explain what their work means to the success of the company.

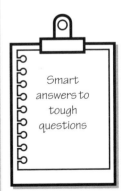

Smart
answers to
tough
questions

---

tions and miraculously the last person to speak will have said exactly what they were about to say. Invite an opinion and they'll agree with yours (until it turns out to be wrong, at which time they'll admit to knowing all along it wouldn't work). Yet they'll claim to have contributed to all your work unit's achievements.

While it may be hard to document their lassitude, you and all their hard-working co-workers know these people aren't pulling their weight. That costs the organization in two ways. First, productivity suffers because their share of the work lags. Second, watching them get away with organizational murder leads to resentment among everyone else, and pretty soon the output of your high performers begins to suffer too.

Smart things to say about motivation

Start with measurable, date-specific individual performance goals.

What to do? Whether you are operating in compliance or commitment mode, a good place to start is to work with such an individual to establish measurable, date-specific performance goals. You'd be amazed at how many people are blissfully unaware of how much more is expected of them. Just setting goals and revisiting them periodically may help a lot.

But let's assume that goal-setting has an impact for about two days – just long enough for your attention to move elsewhere. In traditional compliance mode, you'd discipline the person. That would probably work for another few days. But ultimately, you have three choices: ignore the person's sleepwalking and demoralize the entire work unit; document the now-measurable shortcomings and get rid of the person; or find out the cause of the behaviour and deal with it.

If you choose the third course, before you start trying to motivate this person, make sure it is a motivational issue. Maybe he really doesn't know how to do the job and is very good at hiding that fact. If that's the case, you need to train him, not discipline or motivate him. Or it could be your employee lacks confidence and is frightened of being shown up as inferior. That person needs coaching and counselling, and perhaps an opportunity to work with a mentor until she is convinced she can stand on her own. Since both of these people are probably fearful of making mistakes, they also need assurances that you view mistakes as opportunities for learning, not as capital offences.

It's even possible your absent-on-the-job employee is going through some major personal upheaval off the job and right now just doesn't have the energy left to devote to job tasks. Knowing such facts, you and the person's co-workers might feel differently about covering for her temporarily. Or your organization might have policies and programmes for dealing with such personal issues.

If none of these explain the situation, then 'How can I motivate this person?' really is the correct question. One likely area to focus on is self-esteem. No matter what they indicate, people who chronically shirk usually know in their hearts what they are doing – and it doesn't make them feel good. Even in extreme cases where the culprit pokes fun at the working stiffs and brags about beating the system, deep down this is not a person with a healthy sense of self-worth. This is a person who needs convincing that the work to be done is important and the person who does it is pretty important too.

How come I always have to do the boring work?

All those glamorous dot-com jobs may have fizzled out, but, among those who came of age in the digital heyday, there is still an expectation that work should be constantly creative, exciting and full of ever-changing challenges. Confronted with the fact that much work is repetitive, perfunctory and tedious, the thrill-junkies may get very adept at avoiding what they find dull and mind-numbing. They don't have a self-esteem problem, but they do have a short attention span for what bores them. And those in any technology field have cutting-edge skills they want to hone before they become as obsolete as they perceive their elders to be.

The veterans in the work unit (if there are any) remember that when they came on board, they expected to pay their dues with grunge work for years, perhaps, before they took on anything truly creative. But watching jobs disappear all around them, today's younger workers aren't convinced they'll have such years available to them. And they are convinced they have the knowledge and skills to tackle innovative work now.

KILLER QUESTIONS

Isn't anyone willing to pay his dues any more?

So you probably won't get their willing compliance with talk about paying their dues. If you can show them that the dull tasks are critical to the operation of the organization and that they are divided fairly among co-workers, that will help. If you can make it more fun, say with a pizza and work party to get all that boring stuff done at once, even better. Bribery (in the trade, we call it reinforcement or extrinsic motivation) helps too; so try to reward their completed efforts with interesting assignments.

Missed opportunities

OK, as a manager you can't tolerate it, but you do kind of understand why people avoid doing tedious, repetitive tasks. But how do you explain it – and how do you solve it – when they sit back and let interesting opportunities float right on by without raising a finger to nab one, and even resist when asked to tackle one?

If you ask them why – and you should ask if you find yourself managing one of these work-avoiders – they'll probably respond with some variation of the following:

- I don't have time.

- Nobody's paying me to do that.

- The last time I took on such a project, nobody even said thank you.

Let's look at these one at a time:

- *I don't have time.* There are two possibilities here: either it's true or it's an easy excuse to cover up the real reason. If it's true, then this isn't a motivation problem, it's a time management problem and that's what you need to help the person solve. If it's an excuse, the real reason may be smouldering resentment over perceived treatment that falls into one of the next two categories. Try the question: 'If I could help you solve the time problem, what would it take to get you to do this?'

- *Nobody's paying me to do that.* If Herzberg is right, money isn't a motivator, but the absence of it can be one humdinger of a demotivator. People who are convinced they are underpaid feel undervalued and unappreciated. Refusing to take on new work can be a way of getting back at the organization for this mistreatment. If you can't pay extra for the additional work, you need to find some other way of demonstrating that you and the enterprise hold this person in high regard. Start by asking: 'In lieu of more money, which I can't offer right now, what else I can do to make it worth your while to do this?' And be sure to add, 'I know you are the best person for this job.'

- *The last time I took on such a project, nobody even said thank you.* There it is – that unappreciated feeling again – another mountain-sized demotivator. Again, it helps to find out what show of appreciation would be meaningful to the employee. Try asking, 'How can I show my appreciation in a way that would encourage you to do this?'

There is, of course, one more feasible reason for turning down new opportunities. It is just possible that the employee is perfectly satisfied with the limited role he plays now at work. Perhaps his sole motivation for working at this job is to finance some other part of his life that he cares about much more. What you perceive as an exciting opportunity to him is an unwanted intrusion, maybe even a distraction from his real interest if pursuing it would spill over into his personal time. If that's the case, and he's doing his job within its narrowly defined description, then you may just decide to let him be and find someone else who appreciates these opportunities more.

Mistakes that no one learns from

Except for air traffic controllers and brain surgeons, almost everyone is expected to make mistakes now and then. But we also expect people to learn from their mistakes and improve their performance.

As a customer, I was disappointed but understanding when my new sectional sofa arrived with the arm on the wrong side of one section. Six months later, still without that section, I was enraged when I learned the company had remade it with the same error twice more – which, believe it or not, the spokesperson shared with me, thinking it would placate me! That's when I checked into the store's reputation and found it was notorious for making such blunders. Obviously, nobody there was learning from them. In communications with me, nobody even seemed very concerned about them. Even if the store had a constant flow of new customers to replace all those who would never shop there again, can you imagine the money it was losing by custom-building furniture no one was ever going to buy?

Sometimes it's an individual who, with apparent lack of concern, makes the same mistakes repeatedly. Often it's an entire organization where the *modus operandi* is to push the product out the door at all costs. If you want to change that mindset, you have first to ensure that the organization is not encouraging it. If the enterprise is pushing for greater speed and higher numbers and rewarding managers and workers who accomplish those goals at the expense of quality, then that's the first thing you need to change – not the behaviour of the workers.

Most people prefer to work for an enterprise with a reputation for out-standing quality. They take pride in being part of such an organization. With that in place, it's easier to convince them to demand the same quality of themselves. When they see that by paying attention to the accuracy of their own work they are contributing to the product quality and company reputation, they have good reason to take pride in what they do and make sure they correct their mistakes, not repeat them.

Reducing the costs of low motivation

Add it all up, and low motivation can cost an enterprise big bucks through poor productivity, missed opportunities, rework and disgruntled customers. It can also extract a huge cost psychologically, spreading like ripples and lowering morale.

But it's a price you don't have to pay. You can reduce these costs – even eliminate them – by building six characteristics into each job that reports to you:

1 *Meaningful work.* Even drudge work is worth doing. Just think of the consequences of incomplete forms, grudging service to customers, even dirty bathrooms. People need to know how their efforts contribute to the company's objectives.

2 *Opportunities for growth.* It's not all about promotions any more. Growth can come through acquiring new skills and knowledge, job enrichment and lateral movement.

3 *Sense of control.* Feeling in control is an essential characteristic of adulthood. Any job that withholds control treats employees like children, and that's how they are likely to act (or like rebellious teenagers). If the organization determines the required outcomes, people can experience control over their work by having choices and making decisions about how to accomplish tasks.

4 *Rewarding relationships.* Some people are energized through personal friendships at work. That's not true for everyone, but everyone does need to trust and be trusted, and to experience mutual appreciation and opportunities to learn from others.

5 *Sense of competence.* Through accomplishments, opportunities to use their skills and knowledge, and feedback and appreciation, people develop a sense of their own competence and a desire to demonstrate and expand it.

6 *Recognition and rewards.* We all need reinforcement, to have our competence and our accomplishments confirmed by the recognition of others.

Granted, building these characteristics into each job is easier said than done. That's why Part II of this book is devoted to an in-depth look at each of them.

The smartest things in this chapter

- The best defence against absenteeism is to make coming to work more satisfying than staying in bed or hanging out with friends.

- Even boring tasks can be a source of self-pride if the employee performing them knows they are important to the success of the organization.

- When you can, brighten up repetitious and tedious work by turning it into a work party with everyone pitching in and sharing refreshments.

- The most demotivating aspect of being underpaid is feeling undervalued and unappreciated.

- People take pride in working for organizations known for their outstanding quality, and will monitor and correct their own mistakes.

Notes

1   Deci, E.L. (1995) *Why We Do What We Do*. Putnam, New York (Penguin edition), p.2.

2   Quoted from a personal interview in spring 2002.

Part II
More Than Just a Job

What can a manager do to persuade people to tackle their tasks with vigour and respond to work challenges with energy and enthusiasm? This part of the book is about six job and workplace characteristics that inspire that kind of dedication and commitment. It offers managers suggestions and guidelines for building these characteristics into the work environment of the people who report to them.

Chapter 4 examines what makes work *meaningful*, focusing especially on boosting respect and esteem for routine and repetitive tasks and the people who perform them.

Chapter 5 looks at *opportunities for growth* in an era when upward progress is limited, and growth is less likely to mean promotion and more likely to mean skills building, job enrichment and lateral movement.

Chapter 6 discusses employees' need for a *sense of control* over their own work, and describes how managers can turn over that control without endangering performance quality or their own job security.

Chapter 7 stresses how important *feeling competent* is to employee motivation, and discusses the manager's role in confirming it and improving it.

Chapter 8 addresses how best to use *recognition and rewards* to reinforce high-level performance.

Chapter 9 describes the role *relationships* play in making work worthwhile.

4
Meaningful Work

'When you are working for an organization that has a critical mission, that's crucial to motivation. We keep the stock exchanges running. Our mission and impact are unquestionable, a fact certainly emphasized during the tragedy of 9/11.'

Joseph Meilan, senior vice president, SIAC[1]

'The product we deliver is a wonderful contribution to society. We make it possible for people to fly who could never afford to fly in the past.'

John Denison, executive vice president, Southwest Airlines[2]

Both Southwest Airlines and SIAC enjoy unusually low turnover rates for their industries. One of the things that binds people to each is their conviction that the company they work for has an important purpose. Contributing to that purpose adds meaning to their own lives and generates energy for the work they do.

Commitment to an organization and a job starts with the sense that the work is worth doing. That's got three components. First, does the organization I work for provide a valuable product or service? Second, are my tasks worthwhile, i.e. do they make an identifiable contribution to the mission of the organization? Third, is my work meaningful in the sense that it is personally fulfilling to me?

A big part of a manager's job is helping employees find 'yes' answers to those questions.

Valuable product or service

Some organizational purposes would rank right up there on anyone's list as worthwhile – developing a cure for cancer, for example. Although they are not in the cancer-cure business, recruiters at SIAC and Southwest Airlines have no trouble finding talented people who buy into the importance of their missions – although, in many cases, the same people wouldn't be attracted to both. Farther along the spectrum are companies whose outputs, from shoe polish to hamburgers, seem pretty mundane. Such companies won't wow everyone with the social significance of their products, but with effective communication, they can present compelling cases for meaningfulness, often focusing on factors like:

- People need our product even if it's not glamorous.

- Our quality is the best in its industry.

- We support the community by providing a decent livelihood for our workers.

- Through community outreach we provide various important services.

For managers, a key lesson for motivating employees is that people work more eagerly for organizations they consider important. What people consider important varies from individual to individual. The challenge for managers is to define the organization, its purpose and goals in a way that is meaningful to each employee, demonstrating congruency between the mission of the enterprise and the values, needs and goals of each individual. A speech extolling the virtues of the company may not be enough.

Smart quotes

'People have to understand how what they do contributes to the well-being of humankind.'

Ken Blanchard, Sheldon Bowles, *Gung Ho!* [3]

Worthwhile tasks

There was no clause in the old compliance contract about work that was worth doing. Workers weren't supposed to wonder about that; they were just supposed to do as they were told. But workers do care about it, especially when they are being asked to devote their hearts, souls, bodies and time to their tasks, and too often they get a message that the organization does not consider their work – or, by extension, them – important.

What gives them that message? Their knowledge, or their perception, that:

Smart quotes

'We all wish to be of importance in one way or another.'

From the *Journals of Ralph Waldo Emerson*

- *They are treated with contempt by others in the organization.* In a dairy products plant, a woman whose job was to clean the lunchroom, said plaintively, 'I'd feel better if I knew that my job was important to the company. But I clean off the tables, and they spill things and never wipe them up. I empty the trash bins and clean the floors, and they throw their garbage at the bins and don't even pick it up when they miss. They complain when it's messy, but they are the pigs.'

Tip for managers. The lowliest jobs are often the ones that contribute the most to the comfort and well being of others in the organization. Yet, too often, they receive the least respect. That doesn't happen at companies like the Ritz-Carleton where the mission is customer service, and the method is to value the people who provide it. *Harvard Business Review* editor Paul Hemp wrote of a Ritz trainer, 'He stops to pick up some litter in the hall and puts it in his pocket. "We try to help out housekeeping," he says, "just like they help us when they clean our carts out of the hall."'[4]

- *They are inadequately rewarded, not even thanked.* Here's a logical question: 'If the work were important, wouldn't it be recognized and rewarded?'

  Tip for managers. You may not be able to boost your employees' pay, but you can show your appreciation by telling them how their efforts contributed to an important accomplishment.

> Smart things to say about motivation

We were brought up to show our appreciation by saying 'thank you', so if no one thanks us for our work, it's logical to assume that it was not appreciated and, therefore, not worth doing.

- *No use is made of the work they do.* They write reports no one seems to read, start projects no one follows up on, make great suggestions no one pays attention to. At least, that's the way it looks to workers who never see the results of their efforts.

  Tip for managers. Every organization is looking for ways to cut costs. One place to start is to look closely at all the work done in your work unit and assess its importance. There may be tasks that aren't worth doing and can be eliminated. But, for tasks that are important, make sure the people doing them know why and what becomes of the fruit of their efforts.

- *There will be another reorganization, and everything's going to change anyway.* Reorganization is endemic to many companies. It's no wonder employees feel their work is not worthwhile if it's going to be set aside next month or next year.

  Tip for managers. In the meantime, life goes on. If you can do so honestly, show demoralized employees that their work will have an impact, whatever the future brings. If you are as pessimistic as they are, focus on short-term effects: are they learning something new that they can apply in another context? Are they making new contacts that could be useful later? You might even turn adversity into a motivator: whatever the outcome, let's do this for our own sake, to prove that we can be the best XYZ unit this company has ever had!

- *This whole project is hopeless. It's never going to work.* OK, maybe this is just the whining of a chronic naysayer. Or maybe someone knows something management doesn't.

  Tip for managers. If you give credence to critics' objections, you're half way to getting them to figure out how to make the project work. Even naysayers can often be converted if given a chance to contribute their ideas for how to make the project work better.

Changing the message

To be motivated, employees need to hear a convincing new message – not only hear it, but have it constantly reinforced by the behaviours and attitude of their manager and others in the organization. The new message has to be that:

- the work you do contributes to the objectives of the organization, in clear, specific ways;

- you have specific work goals that are important to the organization, challenging and worthy of your best efforts; and

- as you progress toward your goal, the organization will recognize your accomplishments and provide support in overcoming obstacles.

Smart things to say about motivation

If you want to convince your employees that their work is meaningful, try these suggestions adapted from the book, *Improving Supervisor Productivity Through Motivating Employees.*[5] Just fill in the blanks in the following sentences:

- You are important to this organization because _____
- You are important to this work group because _____
- Other people in the organization rely on you for _____
- I rely on you for _____

How often do you say words like these out aloud to the people who work for you?

Contributing to organizational objectives

It's not just the workers who swab lunchroom floors who wonder how their jobs contribute to organizations' goals. Even contributors to highly visible projects ask themselves sometimes if their efforts are really going to make a difference. Will the fate of the company's goal to increase sales by ten per cent really rise or fall depending upon the completion of a fancy new Web site? Will all these efforts to develop local strategic partnerships make one whit of difference if the company's goal is to expand overseas?

It's hard to stay motivated when you can't see the connection between what you are doing and what the organization wants to accomplish.

Good managers clarify that connection and regularly reinforce it for their employees. They start by keeping the people who work for them updated on the goals and the progress of the organization, relating that information to the work of the unit:

- Here's what the company expects to accomplish … *a ten per cent increase in sales this year. To date we're on target for an eight per cent increase but the goal is still within reach.*

- Here's what we've been asked to contribute … *a new Web site that attracts users to review all our products.*

- Our contribution will affect the organization's success in this way … *our research shows that at least 40 per cent of consumers are getting most of their product information online. It also shows that the more consumers know about each of our products, the more likely they are to upgrade their purchases to the top of our line.*

They also lure employees into helping to develop the work unit's goals and standards and action plan. Goals people set for themselves are almost always more meaningful than imposed goals.

- When can we have the site up and running?

- How many products can we include to start?

- How many hits can we anticipate?

- What do we have to do attract that many hits?

A manager's most critical role in group goal setting and action planning is to ensure the results are neither too easy nor impossibly ambitious. A group that lacks confidence may need some prodding, perhaps a demonstration of confidence on the manager's part that the group is capable of taking on a greater challenge: 'I think we've got the expertise in this room to expand the Web site beyond what you've suggested. What could we add that would make it more compelling to users and more fun for you to create?'

A group that's aggressive and excited might get carried away into pipe-dreams instead of reality. That will get their juices flowing in the short term, but deflate them utterly when their goals prove unattainable and their plans unworkable. Without dampening their ardour, it's the manager's responsibility to ease them back into a level of challenging reality: 'You've just described the dream Web site. Before we reach it, though, we're going to need some quick successes. If we did a first iteration that was less complex but still compelling, what would it look like?'

Finally, turning organizational objectives into meaningful work for individuals requires setting work goals for each employee.

Goals worthy of the effort

Just having a goal makes work more meaningful. Two Motorola assembly line workers motivated themselves by setting their own ever-higher goals to produce more, faster and better. Their supervisor eventually made their jobs even more meaningful, both to themselves and the organization, by challenging them to set a new goal: to teach their methods to their co-workers so everyone would produce at the same high level.

The most worthwhile individual goals derive directly from work unit objectives that clearly contribute to the mission and objectives of the organization. The most meaningful goals come out of a joint goal-setting session, involving employee and manager. The place to start is with the work unit objectives and a discussion of the employee's role in contributing to them.

Smart things to say about motivation

> To be meaningful, goals need to pose a doable challenge. Goals with no stretch quotient fail to energize. Goals that are too hard demoralize because they have failure built into them.

If you are the manager, your most effective tools for this discussion are asking, listening and clarifying. What's least effective is telling – delivering goals you've already set for an employee. But you may need to stimulate an employee who sets personal goals that are less than challenging or rein in, without deflating, one who wants to build a rocket ship and fly to Mars in a day. You'll also need to make sure that, whatever the goals, they include unambiguous standards and measurements so you and the employee will assess progress the same way and agree when the goal has been met. Without clear standards and measurements, a goal is too intangible to get a grip on, and working toward it becomes meaningless.

Questions like these can help you guide a goal-setting session with an employee:

- How would you describe your role in meeting the work unit goals?

- Is there something you feel qualified to do in meeting those goals that is not a part of your current job?

- That's very ambitious. Can you explain how you would accomplish it?

- How would you feel about spreading that over a longer period and committing only to the first part of it now?

- There's a very important role here that I need someone to assume ... How would you feel about taking on that challenge?

- How could I support you if you set a goal to do that?

- What tasks and outputs will you commit to?

- Can you define those so an outsider would know exactly what you meant?

- Can we put numbers and due dates on those?

- Because you have done X, Y and Z in the past, I am confident you could do A, B and C now. Does that seem reasonable to you?

- What support would you need to achieve it?

- Let me be sure I understand you. Here's what you have committed to ... Is that correct?

Assessing and acknowledging progress

Smart quotes

'Cheer the progress, not just the result.'

Blanchard and Bowles, *Gung Ho!*[6]

Few people are as motivated by a goal that's due in a year as by one due in a matter of weeks. It's just a whole lot harder to rev ourselves up when we won't see the results for a long time. Yet most employee and organizational goals are annual ones. You can make those goals powerful motivators all year long if you insist upon establishing periodic milestones – times for mid-course assessment of progress by manager and employee. These milestone discussions are opportunities to:

- *Review the continued relevancy of the goal.* Changes in the organization, the industry, the economy and the market do sometimes render goals and projects irrelevant. You may need to adjust some goals to keep them meaningful for the organization and the employee.

- *Review progress toward goal.* It's a lot easier to assess progress against periodic milestones than to try to figure out if the employee is a quarter or half way toward some far off goal.

- *Celebrate successes.* You don't have to throw a party at every milestone (but don't let me stop you if you want to), but each accomplishment along the way is worth a toast (with coffee if you wish) and a congratulatory note. At work unit staff meetings, make a big deal of milestones achieved, but be sensitive. Despite the common wisdom of praising in public, how effusive you get should depend upon the personality of the employee. Some people are as embarrassed by public praise as they are by criticism. So for those, state their achievements to the larger group without fanfare. Save your accolades for a one-on-one.

- *Analyse problems and determine how to overcome them.* Use mistakes and obstacles as opportunities for learning and for figuring out how to get back on track.

- *Make mid-course corrections in both action plans and the goals.* Whether the action plans need to change to accommodate course corrections or the goals need to change to become more relevant or more realistic, it's a lot more motivating to make those changes midstream than to discover the need for them once it's too late.

When the work is mundane and repetitive

It's dull and boring, but somebody's got to do it. Somebody has to keystroke all those numbers into spreadsheets, all those facts into databases; flip those hamburgers, make those French fries; make those hotel beds; stock those warehouse shelves. There are fewer and fewer assembly line jobs in the knowledge and service-based economies of the West, but there is still a lot of mundane and repetitive work that has to be done.

You may find it hard to describe this work as meaningful, at least not in comparison to open-heart surgery or saving the rainforest, for example. But the key words here are 'has to be done'. In fact, it is the bedrock on which business exists. Woe to the finance executive who turns on his computer and no spreadsheet pops on the screen, the analyst who types in her password, but no database appears. Without its endless supply of uniformly cooked hamburgers, how could a fast-food chain exist?

This dull and repetitive work may not be exciting to perform, but it certainly is needed. As a manager, you can affirm that for the people who do it, giving them a reason for taking pride in what they do.

Give the work and the people who perform it the respect they deserve. The top hotel companies make a religion of doing just that. They recognize that clean rooms and fast, professional service bring customers back. So, while they demand high work standards from their housekeeping and service staffs, they show these workers respect by acknowledging their importance and treating them as professionals.

Give them a broader range of responsibility. The car manufacturers changed their ways years ago. They rearranged their assembly lines so that teams of workers were responsible for making whole cars, rather than every worker endlessly dropping the same part into every car or tightening the same screws over and over again. They also made the workers responsible for quality, giving them the authority to stop the line when something needed fixing. You can make other workers' jobs more meaningful in a similar fashion. You might give a clerical worker primary responsibility for all the work for one client, for example, including client contact as part of the job. Or try building cross-functional teams, giving workers more contact with each other and opportunities to learn each other's jobs.

Here's the unvarnished truth. People take mundane, tedious jobs because they need the money, not because they are looking for meaning in the work. But, for the most part, these jobs don't pay enough money to convince people to stick around and to stay actively engaged over time. If you are managing such a function, and you are not satisfied with high turnover and mediocre performance, figure out how to make these jobs more meaningful for the people who do them.

Smart quotes

"'We're Ladies and Gentlemen serving Ladies and Gentlemen." In terms of human dignity, the argument goes, Ritz Carlton customers and employees are equals. "We're service professionals, not servants.'"

Paul Hemp, *Harvard Business Review*[7]

'But it's not right for me'

Here's an example: I love to read about art restoration. It thrills me to learn about masterworks being returned to their former glory after a disaster like a flood or just years of benign neglect. But if I had to spend my days carefully scraping away the detritus of centuries, I know I'd lose the meaningfulness in the minutia, and if I worked in a laboratory figuring out solutions, the chemicals would be as meaningful as alphabet soup.

Just because the purpose of the task is significant, even momentous, doesn't mean that for every individual the

Smart quotes

'The real job involves facilitating their doing the activities of their own volition, at their own initiative, so they will go on doing the activities freely in the future when we are no longer there to prompt them.'

Edward L. Deci, *Why We Do What We Do*[8]

work is fulfilling. Truthfully, 'not fulfilling' sounds like a whiny, self-pitying excuse, especially if, like art restoration, the job is considered desirable, even prestigious. In response, it's tempting to snort and sputter, 'Then why did you take the job in the first place?' But there are lots of reasonable answers to that: I needed the money; I didn't fully understand what the job entailed; I've changed since I started.

And while it's also tempting to let such a whiner leave – and good riddance – you've probably invested time and money in training the person and you may need his skills. If you want to keep him (mind and body), it's worth it to figure out, with his input, how to make the job more meaningful to him. Some possibilities:

- *Engage the worker in viewing the job through a long-term perspective.* Look at all the career paths this job could ultimately lead to (inside the organization and outside) and determine if one of them would fulfil those unmet needs. Maybe it's worth sticking around until a step in that direction shows up. Do all you can to help the worker prepare for that step.

- *Focus on the technology, not the output.* Help the worker see she's developing skills she can apply to other fields.

- *Adjust the job.* Maybe you can broaden it to include tasks that would be more meaningful to this person.

- *Help him pursue his other interests as an avocation.* If your organization supports not-for-profit causes, you might help him volunteer as a company representative.

- *Best of all, help the person look at his current job through new eyes.* It might not be so alien after all. Cheryl Lazzaro, a managing director in a hi-tech organization, recalls a brilliant technical director who was questioning whether this was the right role for him. But he had been identified as high potential by the company, which was eager to keep him. Taking a chance that he'd leave anyway, the company sent him to a week-long, intensive external leadership development programme. It's the kind of programme, says Lazzaro, where by the third day, either something clicks or the participant turns off. In this case, it clicked.

He came back with a new outlook, having discovered that other individuals were experiencing his same ups and downs and that it was OK to do so. Out of those swings came growth. He also realized that to move up to top management, he didn't have to change who he was and what his values were. In fact, by being himself and sharing some of his experiences, he could help people grow and empower his team. Today, he's a vice president with potential for further movement upward.[9]

Of course, sometimes an individual truly is a square peg in a round hole. If you and the employee have both made every effort to create a better fit, but to no avail, your best service to that person and your organization is to help her find a more appropriate job elsewhere.

'Work exists for man, not man for work,' stated Pope John Paul II in 1988. If that's true, then men and women are certainly entitled to do work they find meaningful. And when they do, motivation takes on a whole new dimension.

The smartest things in this chapter

- People find their work meaningful when the organization provides a valuable product or service, their tasks contribute to the organization's mission and/or their work is personally fulfilling.

- Having a goal makes work more meaningful.

- Periodic milestones generate energy by making long-term goals more immediate.

- People who do dull and repetitive tasks deserve respect for performing work that is crucial to the organization's success.

- You can make work more interesting by broadening the worker's range of responsibilities.

Notes

1   From an interview in summer 2002.

2   Quoted in K. & J. Freidberg (1996) *Nuts!* Bard Press, Austin, TX, p.11.

3   Blanchard, K. & S. Bowles, (1998) *Gung Ho!* William Morrow, New York, p.30.

4   Hemp, P. 'My Week as a Room-Service Waiter at the Ritz' in *Harvard Business Review*, June 2002, p.57.

5   Sussman, L., Herden, R.P. & F.E. Kuzmits *Improving Supervisor Productivity Through Motivating Employees* (1984) Dow Jones-Irwin, Homewood, IL.

6   See note 3, p.147.

7   See note 4, p.56.

8 Deci, E.L. (1995) *Why We Do What We Do*. Putman (Penguin Edition), New York, p.92.

9 From an interview in summer 2002.

5
Opportunities for Growth

Employee growth used to be synonymous with promotion. Ambitious employees pictured themselves in the corner office, running their departments their way, and making decisions that changed the fortunes of the enterprise. That vision propelled them into long, dedicated hours at work.

In studies conducted in the United States, the United Kingdom and Canada in 2001, AON Consulting concluded that growth opportunities were key to employee commitment in all three countries. The conclusions had a slightly different slant for each country, however, expressing what workers want as:

- In the US, 'opportunities for skill growth'.
- In the UK, 'organizations that create and communicate career paths. Employees need to be challenged and trained'.
- In Canada, 'the necessary training and ensuring that there are adequate career advancement opportunities'.[1]

SMART VOICES

At least, that was the baby boomers' vision until about a decade ago when the move toward flatter, leaner organizations began to take the sport out of climbing the corporate ladder. But flatter organizations did not eliminate the possibilities of career growth; they just changed the direction, with more attention to lateral movement. Nowadays, growth equates less to acquiring titles and more to acquiring skills and the opportunities to apply them.

Luckily, that change suits many Generation X workers just fine. They care less about adding new titles and more about adding new skills and challenges, anyway. And it's not just Gen Xers who feel that way; Boomers may be more traditional but they are also adaptive. In 1999, Interim Services Inc., in conjunction with Louis Harris & Associates, published a study entitled *The Emerging Workforce*, which identified a new breed of employee that crossed all age groups, gender and geography. What distinguished these emerging workers from their traditional counterparts was that they were more concerned with gaining new experiences than with having a clear career path.

While traditional employees expected their employers to plot an upward career path for them, emerging workers prefer to collect all those new experiences and, from them, create a career path of their own design. Not that promotions aren't still desirable things; they just aren't the only thing.

Correspondingly, it's been fashionable in the past few years for organizations to extract themselves from the business of creating career paths for employees and to place responsibility for career development in employees' own hands. That makes sense, but it also makes sense for managers to ensure their employees have information, options and guidance available to them, so they can make good development decisions. Whether their eyes are on the next rung up the ladder – contracted though it may be – or on the challenging new project down the hall, people become demoralized and demotivated when they are stuck in their jobs, with no prospects for learning something new, addressing new challenges and expanding their areas of influence. When that happens, performance suffers.

If you are a manager, you can help your employees grow in a host of ways.

Same job, new opportunities

Acquiring new skills and knowledge

Smart quotes

'Most performance and organizational problems are career-related; employees often feel trapped, stagnated, or overlooked in their present jobs or occupations.'

Jerry Gilley, Nathaniel Boughton, Ann Maycunich, *The Performance Challenge*[2]

For infants and toddlers, learning is life. Watch a baby discovering that those wiggling toes and fingers are hers and she can make them do what she wants. Watch a one-year-old pick himself up and toddle off again each time he plops down as he learns to walk – then run and climb – unassisted. Listen to a two-year old consume new vocabulary, taking delight in repeating words of more and more syllables. If, as adults, we had half the energy for learning of the average two-year-old, we'd be unstoppable! But in school we build up resistance to being taught and as grown-ups we're impatient just to *know* without putting time and effort into learning.

Still, even for adults, learning is the basis of all growth. Some people actually enjoy it for its own sake and most people pursue it for the skills and knowledge it bestows. So an opportunity to learn something new can rejuvenate a worn-out worker in a job that no longer poses a challenge. You can generate such opportunities for people who work for you if you:

- *Offer training programmes,* especially for skills they can use to broaden the scope of their work right now, but also to prepare them for future work and to help them better understand the philosophy, processes and systems that drive and support the broad organization. Don't give up on them if your employees don't leap at the chance for new training. Whether they are too bogged down to bother or too full of themselves to think they need it, there's a good chance they'll like it when they try. On the other hand, if employees resist, it may be because they recognize it's not the right training opportunity for them. If you ask them for suggested alternatives, they may come up with something that better meets their needs.

- *Arrange on-the-job-training* through informal apprentice programmes (working closely with an experienced employee in an area that interests the trainee), temporary assignments or job rotations among your staff. Reward your employees for teaching each other their jobs.

- *Appoint your employees to work unit teams* where they will assume some management tasks and to cross-functional project teams where they will be exposed to a variety of functions.

- *Encourage them to take advantage of online training*, especially in technical fields, and tuition reimbursement if your organization has such a programme.

Job enrichment

There's not much point in learning a new skill or a new concept if the worker doesn't get a chance to use it. The training itself, if it's engaging, might be motivating for a while, but the impact will be temporary at best. Eventually, being encouraged to learn something and never given an opportunity to use it might even feel like a betrayal.

Besides, why would you and the organization want to waste all that learning? No appropriate job opening is a very flimsy excuse. With a little imagination combined with some practical thinking, you and the newly skilled employee should be able to come up with some useful ways to apply those skills in his current job. Most job descriptions have enough flex in them to make room for new tasks and responsibilities that tap the employee's full range of skills and insights.

Smart quotes

'There's no magic here. It's not rocket science. People perform better when asked to use their talents, including their brains.'

Terrence Deal and Allan Kennedy, *The New Corporate Cultures*[3]

In his book, *Peak Performance*, Jon Katzenbach tells of an assembly worker at Hill's Pet Nutrition whose real job goes way beyond operating the canned food packing lines to which he is assigned. Although the worker's job description doesn't show it all, his responsibilities include maintaining and fixing the machines; maintaining and purchasing the oils, greases, lubricants and chemicals used in the area, managing a budget of over a quarter of a million dollars; inspecting one of the formulations; and serving as tour guide for the many groups that visit the plant.[4]

Frederick Hertzberg popularized the phrase 'job enrichment' for turning dull and limited jobs into broad and fulfilling ones. His definition of job enrichment included a number of components, including:

- removing controls;

- increasing worker accountability;

- giving a worker a complete unit of work, rather than a single task;

- increasing worker authority;

- increasing information to workers;

- introducing new and more challenging tasks; and

- assigning specialized tasks, allowing workers to become experts.[5]

Hertzberg adamantly distinguished enrichment from job loading, and if you are trying to motivate employees, you should too. It is decidedly not job enrichment to:

- demand more of the same;

- add more dull, routine tasks;

- rotate workers among equally boring tasks; and

- dumb down the job by removing the more time-consuming, difficult tasks.

You might achieve temporary efficiency through job loading, but you won't inspire motivated workers. And even job enrichment has its critics, people who call it exploitation. You may find you have some of those among the very people you are trying to motivate. They are the ones who will grumble that it's all a plot to get them to do additional work for no extra pay. So make sure that enrichment activities are voluntary and that the people who do them get plenty of recognition and visibility throughout the organization.

Looking into the future

Sooner or later, even if her work is interesting, a career-minded person starts to ask herself and her manager, 'Where do I go from here?' If she

Here's a word of advice regarding job enrichment. Without making promises you may not be able to keep, do your best to get those enriched jobs redefined and upgraded. Exciting challenges are powerful motivators, but in time an employee whose job has been broadened but not upgraded may begin to feel resentful and taken advantage of. This is especially a risk if – and we've all seen this happen – the organization brings in new people at higher grades, higher pay, more status and less responsibility. More pay may not, in Herzberg's terms, be a true motivator. But not getting it can be a powerful demotivator, especially to an employee who feels exploited.

Smart things to say about motivation

can't visualize the possibilities, then her current job may begin to feel like a trap. When that happens her interest lags, and probably her productivity does too.

In many organizations there used to be established career paths: an employee could expect to spend X number of years in Job A, then get promoted to Job B, prove herself there, and move on to Job C, etc. But downsizings and reorganizations broke up the paths, and after each disruption, the paths had to be rerouted. Finally, with fewer stations on the hierarchy and greater emphasis on self-management, many companies moved away from formal career pathing for their employees. Many experts agreed that designated career paths were remnants of an old-fashioned, paternalistic style of managing human resources, promoting dependency instead of innovative self-sufficiency. So it was best for employees to make them responsible for managing their own careers.

All true. But managing one's career through the flux of today's ever-changing organizations can be a bewildering task, with options slamming closed just when you are ready to embark on them, and others opening up in unexpected places that you didn't know you had to prepare for. So, formal career paths or not, employees often still need some guidance from someone with a wider perspective.

As a manager, it is part of your job to hold career development discussions with your employees. When you do, make it very clear that the discussion is not about lining up a promotion, it's about *becoming promotable*. That broadens the career scope. While they may focus their aspirations on one or a few jobs, the steps they take to prepare themselves should ready them to move in a variety of directions if their targeted career objective never materializes or their aspirations change.

You may not be able to promise promotions to restless employees who are eager to move on, but you can help them:

- recognize the possibilities and set goals;

- identify the skills and experiences they'll need to pursue their goals;

- figure out how to build relevant skills and gain necessary experience on their current jobs;

- take steps to acquire the prerequisites the current job won't provide; and

- help them gain visibility among people who can assist them in reaching their goals.

Possibilities and goals

Why is it that the earnest probe, 'Where do you want to be in five years?' frequently feels like a trick question to the person on the receiving end? Maybe it's because it often sounds like a question with a right and a wrong answer rather than one inviting a range of responses from the fanciful to the threateningly ambitious. Answer 'president of the company', and the questioner will brush you off as an egomaniac. Say 'in your job,' and you might scare the questioner into sidelining you rather than helping you. Respond 'helping the disadvantaged,' and you'll be tagged as a corporate misfit. 'I'd like to try five different things during that time and see where I fit,' makes you sound indecisive. Every response seems to lead to a minefield, except for the *right* one, whatever that is. So the respondent struggles for an answer that will please the questioner and make a good impression. But it won't necessarily lead to the most motivating career plan.

If you're conducting a career development discussion with an employee, you'll have more success with questions that give credibility to a wider range of answers. For example,

- Can you think of five jobs in this company, any of which you'd like move into in the next few years?

- What about jobs that don't exist here now? If the company could create some jobs for you, what would they be?

- What is it about those jobs that appeals to you?

- Why do you think you'd be good at them?

- What satisfies you most about your current job? Least?

- From what you said about what you like and don't like, I'm wondering if you've ever thought about .... or ....?

- Of all the jobs we've talked about, which would you knock yourself out to achieve?

Of course, if you are conducting such a discussion, there's more to your role than asking questions, although that's a big part of it, since your goal is to guide the employee into making his own career decisions. You should also contribute information you have about the direction the organization is going and what that might open up. Tell the employee anything you know that confirms or contradicts his impression of jobs that interest him. Let him know what fields you think he's particularly good at. Be honest, but sensitive, about those where he's not so good and what he might do to improve.

If it's clear that his aspirations and the possibilities inside the organization don't match, then it's up to you to direct his focus outside without making it sound as if you want rid of him or that he'll be passed over for in-house opportunities. In the current business environment, it makes little sense to demand years of loyalty from a worker. So treat a career goal that's outside the company the same as you would an inside one. Go right on to discuss the skills and experiences he's going to need to reach his goal – wherever that is – and how he can continue to build and hone those within your organization. What you can hope for is a motivated employee who practices *loyalty now* – giving his all to the company he's with before he moves on.

Skills and experiences

Between you, develop a list of the skills and experiences each targeted job calls for. For jobs outside your immediate area, help the employee identify experts who can provide information you don't have. When the list is complete, work with the employee to identify ways to pursue his developmental needs. The training options and job enrichment discussed above are possibilities, and so is another option not yet mentioned here – a lateral job move. Most career paths zig and zag a lot these days, since upward ones are pretty limited. And among the new breed of worker who cares more about job content than title, a lateral move might prove to be the satisfying career change that, temporarily at least, tames the restlessness and calms the itch to move on.

Visibility

You can't plan her career for her; you can't learn new skills for her; you probably can't promise her a promotion. But there's one thing you can do for an employee seeking advancement. You can arrange for her to be very visible to leaders throughout the organization who need to know who she is and what she has done and can do. Take her to meetings with you: send her in your stead occasionally. Send memos to your bosses describing her achievements. Invite your boss and other leaders to a meeting for her to describe some accomplishment. Volunteer her for teams and task forces where she'll meet people who can help her career. Although this paragraph repeatedly says 'her', as if suggesting you single out a specific employee for this special treatment, you should be doing this for all your employees who have accomplished something you are proud of. It might boost not only their motivation, but yours too.

Smart quotes

'Advancement is the result of a successful mix of three characteristics: competency, visibility, and opportunity.'

Florence Stone and Randi Sachs, *The High-Value Manager*[6]

The smartest things in this chapter

- Reorganizing and downsizing has reduced opportunities for promotions, but not for learning and applying new skills.

- Learning opportunities include training programmes, on-the-job training, team participation and online training.

- Job enrichment allows employees to learn and apply new skills without leaving their current jobs.

- Career paths are less predictable these days, but employees still want to anticipate, 'Where do I go from here?'.

- Helping an employee become visible to upper management opens up more career opportunities for that person.

Notes

1   Source: www.aon.com.

2   Gilley, J.W., N.W. Boughton & A. Maycunich (1999) *The Performance Challenge*. Perseus, Cambridge, MA, p.197.

3   Deal, T.E. & A.A. Kennedy (1999) *The New Corporate Cultures*. Persus, Cambridge, MA, p.272.

4   Katzenbach, J. (2000) *Peak Performance*. Harvard Business School Press, Boston, pp.208–9.

5   Herzberg, F. 'One more time: How do you motivate employees?' in *Harvard Business Review*, September–October 1987, p.114 (reprinted as an HBR Classic from the January–February 1968 issue).

6   Stone, F.M. & R.T. Sachs (1995) *The High-Value Manager*. AMACOM, New York, p.206.

6
Sense of Control

At some time in your life you've probably had both kinds of jobs: there's the kind where you are given a very specific task, exact instructions for performing it, and a clear warning not to deviate from prescribed methods. Then there's the other kind, where you had an objective to meet or a problem to solve, and you decided how to do it. Which one got your juices flowing?

Like you, your employees will be a lot more turned on by work they control than by following orders.

'I planned each charted course; Each careful step along the byway, But more, much more than this, I did it my way.' From the song 'My Way'. The smart voice was Sinatra's.	SMART VOICES

Putting employees in charge of their own work means giving them decision-making power and control over the resources necessary to carry out those decisions. That's scary for many managers because they see it not as expanding control, but as giving up their own. Doing that, they fear, leaves them wide open to:

- suffering for other people's mistakes if things go wrong; or

- becoming unnecessary themselves if things go right.

Smart quotes

'How many times do we intentionally or unintentionally cage our company's eagles? How many times do we say "you're empowered, you're empowered" only to slam shut the cage door with "be sure to follow all the checklists [*slam*] and don't spend over $15 without prior approval [*slam*] and don't change the work schedule [*slam*] and ..."'

Jim Harris, *Getting Employees to Fall in Love with Your Company*[1]

That sounds like a lose/lose proposition. But it needn't be like that. Turning over control isn't about being blamed for others' mistakes; it is about enjoying the glory of their successes. Imagine a senior executive saying, 'Oh, we might as well get rid of Jane. All she ever does is develop her people so they can do their work without her.' Sounds pretty ludicrous, doesn't it? Organizations don't punish managers for developing their people, they reward them for it. Plus, in today's lean enterprises, there are always plenty more things to do for a manager who is freed up from the day-to-day oversight of employees' projects.

So for the manager, what looks like lose/lose is really win/win. For the employee, the big win is the motivational impact of having a sense of control.

To feel they are in control, people need to:

- have choices of what to do and how to do it;

- create their own work processes;

- have authority to make decisions; and

- know they can take initiative and be innovative.

As a manager, you can make those things possible for your employees.

Having choices

From determining broad organizational objectives to deciding who gets a report or what colour ink to use, work is a series of choices. The more choices employees make for themselves, rather than having them inflicted on them by someone else, the more dedicated they will be to ensuring a successful outcome.

Smart quotes

'Perhaps there is an innate or *intrinsic* need to feel a sense of personal autonomy or self-determination ... That would imply that people need to feel that their behaviour is truly chosen by them rather than imposed by some external source.'

Edward Deci, *Why We Do What We Do*[2]

- *Choices at the work unit level.* You'll get more employee commitment to unit goals if you invite employees to participate in making choices for the whole work unit. Your unit probably has some directives imposed from above, things like cut costs by 25 per cent or increase production by 10 per cent or add a new product line (and don't you wish you had been invited to participate in determining those?). But you've still got plenty of choices to make: what to do to cut costs, how to increase production, what steps to take and when to take them to add the new product line. When you invite employees to help you choose the best paths to take, you not only increase their commitment to unit success, but you benefit from their range of expertise and hands-on knowledge.

- *Choices at the individual level.* Giving employees choices begins with setting individual performance goals – normally a joint employee–manager effort. If, as the manager, you reiterate the organizational purpose and the work unit goals and invite the employees' input into what they can do to contribute, you are letting them make choices. Of course, it is also your role to explain your expectations of them and any special needs you have for their skills and expertise. Providing choices doesn't mean giving workers freedom to decide not to do what you expect. It does mean letting them decide how to go about meeting your needs.

Creating processes

Workers everywhere feel trapped by inefficient processes they didn't create and see no hope for changing. Organization and training consultant Rosalind Gold has been helping people battle the debilitating 'The boss won't let me do it differently' syndrome for a long time. One of her first memories of it dates back to an early job on a business publication. 'I was sitting across from a clerk who just gotten hired full time after working as a temp', she recalls. 'One day she looked so gloomy I asked her what was wrong. She said she had to add up a bunch of numbers and send them upstairs, but that the people upstairs really should be doing the addition. When I asked why she didn't just send up the numbers, she replied, "Oh, I couldn't."' So Gold suggested she call the people upstairs and ask. They readily agreed to take the raw numbers. 'They were number crunchers anyway. By giving them the numbers in raw form, it lessened the chance of error and speeded up turn-about time.'

By one improvement in the process, the clerk gained time she could spend on parts of her job she found much more rewarding. Why was she doing it the old way? Because, says Gold, 'Somebody had made it part of her job and she felt she couldn't change it.'

Rightly or wrongly, people are often convinced that their bosses won't let them make changes. For a trainer, it's always disconcerting to hear workshop participants insist, 'My boss wouldn't let me do it that way', when it was their bosses who sent them to the programme in the first place. Gold, who specializes in business communication and project management, took that on once when she was conducting a business writing programme for an insurance company. The purpose of the workshop was to teach participants to write user-friendly letters that insurance customers could understand without having to call the company for an explanation. Participants complained that their supervisors frequently demanded they rewrite their letters before sending them out. Yet they were convinced those same supervisors would object if they applied the techniques they were learning in class. They were mired in helplessness.

Gold's response was to help them line up ammunition to convince their supervisors to buy into the new writing approach. 'I asked for numbers,' she recalls, 'how many letters were returned, how long it took to correct them, how much it cost. I got agreement that it would save a considerable amount of time and money if supervisors would support them. It would benefit everybody. Then we got into how to set up a session with their supervisors to brief them. We talked about what would be the first step, the second step and so on, always focusing on the goal. The mood definitely shifted. Now they felt like there was something they could do, and they went back and did it.'

You may have employees who just need loosened reins to start creating new processes and improving old ones. Or you may have people working for you who are so conditioned to doing as they are told that they can't imagine having the freedom to find a better way. You can help those people along, as Gold did, by encouraging them to set goals and then clarify doable steps. 'Small steps', says Gold, at least to start. 'Nothing big.' Put together, those steps become new processes that will energize the people who created them.[3]

Making decisions

In his book, *Peak Performance*, Jon Katzenbach quotes Sally, an associate in a Home Depot store: '[Sure], you have to decide at some point whether making the customer happy is best for the company or just best for the customer ... Every customer will test your limits [to see] how far ... you are willing to go. But ... [management] feels they can trust me with the decision.'[4]

Home Depot experienced phenomenal growth by imbuing its associates with a passion for customer service and then freeing them to decide, day by day, how best to provide it.

Home Depot's management knows the secret shared by well-run companies everywhere: the best decisions are made by people closest to the action.

As customers, we're delighted when a front-line person in any organization makes a decision to do something extraordinary for us without going through several tiers in the hierarchy to get an approval first. It saves us so much time and aggravation. Now think of the time and aggravation to be saved in any enterprise by granting all its associates similar decision-making authority in their work. Contracts would be signed faster; projects would be started sooner and perhaps completed on time more often. Glitches in any process would be resolved more quickly and probably more effectively. And employees' morale and commitment would soar.

Yet it's hard for many managers to trust their employees to make good decisions, so they insist on having all new questions and unexpected situations brought to them for resolution. Why? They've got plenty of excuses. Here are some samples:

- *The employee doesn't have all the pertinent information.* Well, why not? Why are employees left in the dark about things that affect their work? That doesn't serve the organization well at all, and it's easy to resolve. Give them the information.

- *I'm accountable, so I need to make the decision.* So is the CEO accountable to the board of directors and the board members accountable to shareholders. But they delegate decision making, so why shouldn't a work unit manager? You don't need to make each decision; you just need to be kept in the loop when a decision is made.

- *The employee isn't experienced enough to make such decisions.* Organization development consultant, William Becker of Strategic Business Resources, says there is truth to this. 'Young people today are better educated and know more than we did,' he asserts. 'They can go on the Internet and get information it took somebody 30 years to learn about. They read it and think they can apply it, but without the understanding that comes with experience, they can't anticipate the possible variety of results and therefore the consequences of their actions.' Yet with change happening so fast, he adds, there's no time to show them the ropes the old-fashioned way, one step at a time over the years. Instead, managers need to focus on helping their impatient employees acquire critical thinking skills so they are ready to make decisions in short order. Becker's recommendations to managers for how to do that include:
  - Train employees in problem solving and critical thinking skills.
  - Involve them in real job problems and strategies, providing opportunities to apply those skills individually, in work unit teams, and in task forces.
  - Brush up on your own coaching skills so you can coach your employees through the learning process.
  - Bring employees into management problem-solving discussions.

They'll get a flavour of how to apply the skills and a better understanding of the potential results of their decisions.
- Involve people in the business side of the business: finance, marketing, budgeting, sales, strategy, customer contact, etc. They'll learn and get a reality check at the same time.

- *I encourage them to make their own decisions, but they keep bringing their problems to me.* What's driving that behaviour, fear of punishment perhaps? Employees have to be allowed to make mistakes and learn from them. But if coming to you for a decision is just a habit, don't let them get away with it. Ask them, 'What would you do? Why is that the best decision? How will it handle x, y and z?'. Prod them into digging deeper into the situation before finalizing their decision if you think they are missing something. Finally, sanction their decision (even if it's not quite the one you would have made) and provide your support to make it work.

SMART VOICES

'One of the things that causes powerlessness is that people themselves don't want to take risks because the organization punishes mistakes rather than learning from them.'

Michael Maccoby[5]

Taking initiative

Most companies have something in their values statements about innovation and initiative. So let's start with the assumption that your organization really does want its employees to show initiative and allows them freedom to do so. All the evidence shows that such freedom is motivating. If your employees are choosing not to exercise it, then that's a paradox worth investigating.

In some companies, an employee with a great new idea pulls together a team, successfully petitions management for necessary funding, and goes to work making the idea a reality. In a Motorola plant, for example, the walls are lined with photographs of teams that originated and performed like that.

In other companies, people keep their ideas to themselves or swap stories among each other about 'What I'd do if I were in charge'. But talking about ideas that way doesn't make them happen. In fact, it's more likely to reinforce workers' conviction that 'they' never listen to 'us', a perception that squashes any motivation to try something new and innovative on one's own volition.

The only way to change that perception is to start listening – with full attention. The next time one of your employees complains about a slow-moving process, an inferior tool or technology, a chronic problem, or a policy that hinders work efforts, tune in instead of off, no matter how often you've heard the same tale of woe. Elicit the employee's ideas for improvement and pay those ideas the respect of taking them seriously. Instead of brushing off comments that sound outrageous, ask questions to clarify fuzzy thoughts, temper fantastic ones and extract workable ideas. You may get a shrug or 'that's management's job' the first time you try this, but as you hone your questioning skills and really pay attention to the answers, you'll get better and better responses. Who can resist someone who really wants to know what they think? Try questions like these:

- What are we doing wrong that is causing that?

- What do you think we should do differently?

- How would that take care of the problem?

- What about .... ? How would your suggestion resolve it?

- What impact do you think that might have on other parts of the organization?

- Do you know any other company that is doing something like this?

- Could you check with them and get their experience?

- What one change would have the biggest impact?

- How long would it take?

- Could we start by piloting it in .... ?

- What would the first step be?

If taking innovative action is new to your employees and to you, encourage them to start small. You might ask, 'To begin, what would be the smallest step with a significant impact?'. It would be more comfortable for all of you, and as they rack up successes, you'll find it easier to approve riskier projects and they'll find it easier to tackle them.

Supporting success

If you wonder what you're going to do after you delegate all that control to your employees, don't worry. Your job won't disappear. In fact, it will expand. They are still going to need you, not to tell them what to do, but to create an environment in which they can succeed and all of you can advance to new challenges.

When you transfer control of their work to your employees, your job changes from directing to supporting. Keep in mind the words of Max DePree, who wrote the most poetic (and realistic) management book ever, *Leadership Is an Art*: 'The first responsibility of a leader is to define reality. The last is to say thank you. In between the leader must become a servant and a debtor.'[6] If the retired CEO of Herman Miller, one of the world's most admired companies, was content to be a 'servant,' you can do it too – as he meant it: providing people with what they need to succeed.

What empowered employees need

To take control of their jobs, employees need their managers to give them:

- *A clear purpose* – what the enterprise needs from them, why it's important, how it connects to the mission and goals of the organization.

- *Clarity on the limits* to their authority to make decisions – and the assurance that within those limits the choices are theirs. But this isn't a one-time, set-in-stone thing. Employees also need to know what it would take to convince you to broaden their fields of authority. The dialogue should be ongoing, covering, as Kenneth Thomas says, 'Here's where you are now, what you can do without coming to me for approval. I know you'd like to do .... too, but you're going to have to show me first. So here's what I need you to do ...'[7]

- *Information* they need to make effective decisions. Keep them up to date on things like upcoming organizational changes, legal issues that might affect them and what the competition is doing.

- *Opportunities* to work on organization-wide projects where they can learn how decisions are made throughout the enterprise and build up a network they can reach out to. Recommend them for project teams. Make an employee your assistant/surrogate on projects you work on.

- *Visibility* within top management circles and among your peers, so they'll have credibility throughout the organization. Take them to meetings you attend and arrange for them to describe their own projects to people who can cut through obstacles for them.

SMART VOICES

'Empowerment would be a disaster if people assume that means abdicating oversight. Your purpose really is to bring people along to the point where they are self-managing.'

Kenneth Thomas[8]

- *Coaching* on everything from technical issues to politicking.

- *Feedback* on how they are doing, which means you'll need to set up a regular system for them to report their progress. Encourage them to discuss problems frankly before they become insurmountable obstacles. But don't take it upon yourself to solve their problems for them. Instead, be a sounding board and a facilitator to guide them into identifying and implementing their own solutions.

The magic trick for the manager is to provide all those things without micro-managing. It's so easy to grant all that authority to an employee and then take it away, bit by bit, by taking over in a crisis, hovering, punishing mistakes, or just making suggestions that carry the weight of orders. It's tough for traditional managers to avoid micromanaging, and it's even tougher for superhero managers brought in to jump-start moribund work units.

Karen Massoni, an organization development consultant and executive coach in New York, describes a manager whose instincts to jump in and solve problems unilaterally are beginning to erode the energy and motivation he worked hard to instil among his direct reports. 'In this instance,' Massoni explains, 'the manager has done an amazing job. He took over a mismanaged, ineffective unit, cleaned house and handpicked his people. He then made a major commitment in both time and money to develop his organization into a stable, cohesive team. People were given the responsibility to set business objectives in line with the department's overall strategic goals. In an organization that had been in chaos, people welcomed his style of leadership. For the most part, they are motivated, love their jobs, and will do anything he asks.'[9]

But some chinks are beginning to appear in the solidarity and spirit of the group. With 9/ll and current economic, industry and market-place challenges, Massoni has noticed that the manager's take-charge persona is going into hyperdrive.

'In some cases, he's making decisions alone and wresting responsibility and authority from the people who report to him,' she says. 'His style is to demand, "You gotta get it done, you gotta get it done," but not to set deadlines. Then when a situation turns into a crisis, he'll unilaterally do something like bring in a consultant to take over. I'm beginning to see people questioning their own competence and getting demotivated.'

If you start to get hints from your employees that they resent your intrusion into their domains, work with them in a team or one-on-one to clarify:

- where they want you to back off;

- what you need from them to make you comfortable doing that;

- your expectations in terms of outcomes and schedule; and

- a reporting/feedback system that meets both your needs.

Effectively turning control over to employees means giving it to the people closest to the situation, people in the position to make the best decisions. And while, yes, you will need to let them make some mistakes and learn from them, nobody – least of all your employees – is asking you to sit by and watch them make fatal blunders that will bring down the wrath of senior management on their head and yours.

The smartest things in this chapter

- The more choices employees make for themselves, the more dedicated they will be to ensuring their efforts have a successful outcome.

- Workers often feel trapped in processes they assume they are helpless to change.

- Managers who trust their employees to make decisions save time for themselves and their customers while boosting their employees' morale and commitment.

- Even in risk-averse organizations, managers can encourage innovation by helping employees assess their ideas and develop the best ones, one step at a time.

- When employees control their own work, the manager's job is to provide what they need to succeed.

Notes

1   Harris, J. (1996) *Getting Employees to Fall in Love with Your Company*. AMACOM, New York, p.98.

2   Deci, E.L. (1995) *Why We Do What We Do*. Putnam, New York (Penguin edition), p.30.

3   From an interview in summer 2002.

4   Katzenbach, J.R. (2000) *Peak Performance*. Harvard Business School Press, Boston, p.135.

5   From an interview in spring, 2002.

6   DePree, M. (1989) *Leadership Is an Art*. Doubleday, New York, p.9.

7   From an interview in spring 2002.

8   Ibid.

9   From an interview in summer 2002.

7
Feeling Competent

Let's say you are offered a choice of two important projects. One of them you know you could do well. You've got the knowledge and the skills, and this is an excellent opportunity to apply them. The other one you aren't so sure you'd shine at. You've been involved in similar projects in the past with mixed results. You wonder if you would know what to do or how to do it in order to succeed. Which are you likely to choose?

Smart quotes

'Research has found that every person can do at least one thing better than any other 10,000 people!'

Dean R. Spitzer, *Supermotivation*[1]

Well, some people just can't resist impossible challenges, but most likely you answered that you'd choose the project you felt competent to handle. Most of us are a lot more motivated to do work we expect to succeed at than work we fear we might not do well.

Motivational psychologist Edward L. Deci points out that competence is important for both extrinsic and intrinsic motivation. People have to feel competent to perform the behaviours necessary to earn rewards. And feeling competent adds to the enjoyment of the activity itself.[2]

There is a difference, however. Someone else judges our competence and determines whether or not to reward our performance. Our enjoyment of the activity depends upon how we judge our own competence. But for many of us maybe there's not so much difference after all, because to a degree we judge ourselves through others' eyes. To feel confident, we need to have our own positive assessment confirmed by others. Feedback and appreciation affirm our often shaky confidence in our own skills and abilities.

Most of us would be satisfied to generalize the obvious, 'We all need to feel competent. We would rather do something we can do well than something we're really bad at.' But researchers/scholars like Edward Deci aren't content with that. They have to prove it empirically. Deci arranged an experiment to test the theory that competence affects intrinsic motivation. He gave two groups of subjects puzzles that looked very similar. What you couldn't tell just by looking at them was that one group's puzzles were pretty easy and the other group's quite difficult. So, working on tasks that appeared the same, one group succeeded relatively well and the other group failed miserably. As Deci expected, 'those who received evidence of their own competence were subsequently more intrinsically motivated than those who saw evidence of relative incompetence.'[3]

Satisfying the need

Deci also recognized from his experiments and observations that doing easy tasks well doesn't satisfy our need for competence. We need what he calls optimal challenge, something tough enough to give us a feeling of accomplishment.

Satisfying the need for competence takes a variety of forms among different people:

- *Seeking ever greater challenges to conquer.* Some people keep upping the ante for themselves. As soon as they are competent at one task, they need to take on another. Once they've climbed Denali, they have to tackle Everest. When they've scaled Everest, they have to do it again without oxygen.

  Tip for managers. If you've got a 'mountain climber' on your staff, don't expect her to continue to be motivated by repetitive work no matter how demanding it is and how good she is at it. She's going to need constant new challenges to prove her competence to herself over and over. Encourage her to set higher goals and go after them.

- *Sticking with what they are good at.* This is just the opposite to those who need higher and higher mountains to climb. Deci gives the example of a rewrite man on a newspaper who was extraordinarily good at what he did. His job gave him so much satisfaction that he turned down a promotion to editor.[4]

  Too many skilled technicians get pushed into management, where their technical competencies mean little and the required new competencies are foreign to them. It's a move that is demotivating to them and to the people who work for them.

  Tip for managers. If you are managing an expert technician, count your blessings. But don't assume that just because he's feeling good about himself and his work now, that happy situation will continue indefinitely. After he's solved every variety of problem his job has to offer, his eyes may glaze over and his motivation lag until he, too, gets a chance to reinforce his feelings of competence with an 'optimal challenge'.

KILLER QUESTIONS

What can I do to motivate an employee who resists trying anything new?

- *Fear of appearing incompetent.* This insidious driver of human behaviour can lead to all sorts of unproductive behaviour, including avoiding new experiences or new ways of doing work, resisting new assignments, shunning new technology, covering up mistakes and shying away from anything competitive. This is the dark side of the need for competence, which instead of motivating people to do a job well, shackles them in a confining space that inhibits them from growing and increasing their abilities. Sadly, their reluctance to learn and do new things may ultimately brand them with the label they fear most: incompetent to handle inevitable changes.

An employee is not likely to confess to her manager, 'I don't want to take that assignment because I'm afraid I won't do well and I'll look stupid and be embarrassed.' Instead, she's more likely to protest that she's too busy with her current workload, that there is no one available to take over her ongoing work, or that the new project has no chance of working and would be a waste of time. It takes a little mind-reading to decipher that none of those excuses is really what's stopping her, nor is she just lazy, but rather she is afraid. And even if you figure it out, your reassurances may not win her over. If you tell her you are confident she can do it, she may become additionally apprehensive that she'll let you down personally if she fails. If you tell her to go ahead and try it, you'll see she gets all the help she needs, and she won't be punished if she fails, then you might just convince her that you, too, think she probably won't succeed.

Tip for managers. What will help is to show her the connections between what she's done successfully in the past and the new assignment you'd like her to take on, suggests consultant/coach Karen Massoni. Say something like, 'The reason I'm asking you to do this is because it requires the ability to ...., which you demonstrated when you did ....' You might also give her a choice of new challenges, some less intimidating than others. As she enjoys some successes and the new feelings of competence they provide, she'll become more confident about trying something more challenging. And if she does fall short of her own expectations once or twice and discovers that you and her peers don't then treat her with disdain, she'll release some of the old qualms. Of course, if you punish her for not living up to your expectations, you'll redouble her fears.

Proving competence

If you are working on a puzzle, proving competence is pretty straightforward. Either you solve it or you don't. At work, it's not always that clear-cut. We need satisfactory evidence that we've done a first-rate job and are entitled to feel good about it. We also need to satisfy some other judge that we've completed our tasks satisfactorily and are competent to take on more challenges of this kind.

Competence is confirmed by successful accomplishment of tasks. That calls for standards and measurements – objective evidence that we've met our own and others' expectations.

Competence is easy to judge when success is measured by numbers – units produced, deals closed, sales made, money earned, deadline dates met, errors made. As long as everyone is using the same numbers to measure by, both the individual performing the work and outsiders judging it should make the same assessment.

But a lot of competencies are not so readily measured by numbers, although we often try. To confirm my competence as a trainer, for example, at the end of a workshop I might give participants an evaluation sheet and ask them to rate me on a scale of one to five. If my scores average 3.9, I'll feel barely competent the next time I run that workshop. If I average 4.6, I'll feel comfortably confident in my own ability, and if I get a 4.9, I'll feel more than competent. I'll gloat.

But training is about transferring knowledge and skills so that participants take them back to their workplaces and apply them to the benefit of themselves and the organization. Do those evaluation scores tell me anything about my competence there? Not really. They merely told me how competent I was at holding participants' attention and giving them a positive experience.

If we define competence in terms of quality, impact and outcomes, it gets a lot harder to put numbers on, but employees still need standards they can point to and say – to the agreement of everyone – 'I achieved that; therefore I am competent at doing tasks of this kind.'

Smart quotes

'We measure what is easier to measure, rather than what is important.'

Geoffrey Bellman, *The Consultant's Calling*[5]

Identifying those standards is best done as a joint employee–manager undertaking, and the most effective time to do it is before the employee embarks on a new project or task. If you are a manager working with an employee to set competency standards for tasks you can't put numbers on, hold a discussion around questions like these:

- What outcomes have to happen?

- What will we observe that will confirm they have happened?

- Whom do you have to satisfy?

- What do they need? (If neither of you know, the employee should ask.)

- How will we know you have met that need?

And if you want your employee to succeed in developing a new competency, be sure to ask:

- What can I do to assist you and make sure those outcomes occur?

Confirming competence

There are lucky people so supremely self-confident that they need only their own assessment of their competence. But most of us feel a lot more secure when our positive self-assessment is reflected in feedback and appreciation from others. That is, in fact, one of the reasons that financial rewards have a motivating effect. It's not just that we want the extra money to go shopping with, but also that the reward is a tangible expression of the organization's appreciation. It confirms our fragile self-assessment that we did a good job. (There is much more about rewards in general and money in particular to come in Chapters 8 and 10.)

One obvious way to provide positive feedback and show appreciation is to praise people for their work. Praise elevates people's confidence in their competence – or so we would assume. But psychologist Deci and his colleagues did some experiments to test the effects of praise on intrinsic motivation and discovered that the impact of praise was more complicated than we might think. In some cases, praise actually seemed to undermine intrinsic motivation.

Based on these experiments, Deci offers this advice: If you want to boost someone's pleasure in their work, avoid praise that suggests shoulds, expectations, or comparisons – phrases like 'living up to expectations,' or 'doing as you should'. Instead, keep your praise simple – 'You've done very well.'[6]

It seems that when people hear shoulds and expectations, their mental reaction is 'You're saying this to get me to do more work.' This kind of praise is perceived as trying to control the person who is receiving it. The message is that the whole point of the work is to live up to someone else's expectations. It diminishes the person's pure enjoyment of doing the task and becoming more competent.

Don't let Deci's experiments frighten you away from providing positive feedback. Just do your best to keep your praise message one of pure appreciation for the job done. Don't dilute it with a subliminal 'you're only doing what I expected of you'. There are more motivating ways of encouraging employees to continue to apply their skills to the necessary work of the organization.

Exercising and increasing competence

If I'm an employee feeling good about my own competence, I'm not going to want to sit on it. I'm going to want to use it, show it off and build upon

SMART VOICES

Some feedback you never forget. It doesn't have to be extravagant to make an impression.

Consultant Rosalind Gold describes an occasion when she was an editorial assistant at the American Management Association. 'I was sitting at my desk proofreading, immersed in my task. The head of the department, Patricia Haskell, walked by and stood in front of my desk. I don't know how long she was there. Finally I looked up.

'"You really concentrate," she said. Thirty years later I still remember. Since then, I've prided myself on my ability to concentrate. Having somebody recognize a strength is very motivating.'[7]

it. I am going to want new opportunities to use the skills and knowledge I've acquired.

As a manager, you can provide such opportunities for the people who report to you:

- Enrich employees' jobs to take full advantage of all their competencies.

- Encourage employees to suggest new projects that build on their competencies and contribute to the work unit's goals.

- Recommend employees for cross-functional project teams that require their competencies, especially teams that will not only use the skills they have but give them opportunities to develop new ones.

- Lend employees (or a portion of their time) to other work units that require their skills.

- Describe their successes to your boss and others in the organization who may know of other opportunities to apply the same skills, or create opportunities for them to report on their accomplishments themselves.

Bad news that makes you feel good

I know some people who truly like getting corrective feedback. They are delighted to be informed of every tiny error in their work, every less-than-perfect behaviour or outcome. Unlike the less secure among us, they don't interpret these comments as criticism; they see them as gifts – opportunities to improve that they'd get no other way.

Those of us with more fragile egos bruise a little when our manager or a colleague says something negative about our work. So, I admit, the subhead about bad news that makes us feel good was a bit of hyperbole. But delivered sensitively, constructive feedback can inspire us to improve, and we do feel better when know our competence has increased.

When you've got to address an employee's poor performance, these guidelines lead to positive outcomes:

1   *Investigate the situation first.* Be sure you have the full picture. You don't want to discover afterward that the employee you yelled at for coming in late just took a sick child to the hospital. Or that it really was a computer crash that scrambled all the numbers on the spreadsheet.

2   *Choose a quiet and private place.* Public criticism is demeaning to the receiver and embarrassing to everyone else who hears it.

3   *Criticize the behaviours or the outcomes, not the person.* 'How could you be so stupid?' seldom inspires a useful response.

4   *Describe very specifically both the expected performance and the unacceptable performance.* For example, 'I need you to stay at your telephone continuously except for authorized breaks. Yesterday you were away for three 20-minute periods.' Then explain why the expected performance is necessary: 'For every three customers who call and cannot get through immediately, we lose one order.'

5   *Listen more than you talk.* A feedback session should be a two-way conversation. Ask the employee to tell you what is causing the variance between expected and actual performance, and listen without interrupting. Ask also what you can do to help.

6   *Acknowledge the employee's point of view.* You don't have to agree with it; just paraphrase what the employee says, then guide the comments away from past mistakes and toward future improvement.

7   *Encourage the employee to determine the solution.* People are motivated by their own decisions. Make suggestions if necessary to keep the discussion on target, but avoid dictating a solution if possible.

8   *Schedule a follow-up discussion.* This puts teeth in your expectations, without being threatening. And you can use it for acknowledging improvements or for fine-tuning the employee's efforts if necessary.

While it's happening, constructive feedback may not feel real good to the recipient (except for those few unusual friends of mine). But if you follow the steps above when you deliver it, it can lead to much better feelings later when the problems are corrected and the employee's feelings of competence are confirmed.

There's an axiom about giving negative feedback: do it privately. But every rule has its exception. This one may fall under the category of 'don't try this at home (or in your office)'. But it's a revealing illustration of how different approaches can motivate different people.

Florence Stone, editorial director at the American Management Association, tells this story about one of her first jobs, working as an associate editor for the American Gas Association. 'I wrote an article and handed it to my boss. He burst out laughing and said "This is the worst lead I've ever read." Not only did he tell me, he told the managing editor. We had an open office and were right out where everyone could see and hear us. Then he handed it back and told me to do it over. Did it motivate me? Sure, it taught me how to write a succinct lead. To this day I'm grateful.'[8]

SMART VOICES

But if they are not competent, what then?

Chronically poor performers, the people you'd most like to light a fire under, don't get much motivational spark from feeling competent. But the pleasure of feeling competent is theirs to enjoy as they start building their skills and improving the outcomes of their work. It probably won't help much to tell them, 'Look, you're really going to like this job a lot more if you'll just knuckle down and learn to do it right.' There are more effective ways of helping workers improve their competence.

- Let them choose one area of improvement on which to focus. Giving them this choice taps into their need for control, a motivator in itself.

- Reinforce the importance of the tasks they do, how they contribute to the purpose and objectives of the organization. Remember, being competent at trivial tasks isn't particularly motivating.

- To help employees learn from mistakes, use constructive feedback. Invite the employee to explain why the mistake happened and suggest ways to keep it from happening next time.

- Provide training and on-the-job coaching.

- Reinforce successful application of new skills with non-controlling praise: e.g. 'You fixed my computer virus problem very well.' Avoid the insinuation that 'You are finally living up to our requirements.'

- Look for opportunities for the employee to exercise new competence in performing tasks.

Move on to another area for improvement. The employee might just enjoy this new feeling of competence enough to want to increase it.

The smartest things in this chapter

- To feel competent, some people need to meet ever greater challenges.

- Others feel more competent when they stick to what they know they do well.

- Employees need standards by which to measure their competence.

- Most of us need to have our feelings of competence confirmed by others.

- Delivered sensitively, constructive feedback can help people improve their competence.

Notes

1   Spitzer, D.R. (1995) *Supermotivation*. AMACOM, New York, p.73 (based on D.O. Clinton & P. Nelson (1992) *Soar with Your Strengths*. Delacorte, New York).

2   Deci, E.L. (1995) *Why We Do What We Do*. Putnam, New York (Penguin edition), p.64.

3   Ibid, p.66–7.

4   Ibid, p.64–5.

5   Bellman, G.M. (1990) *The Consultant's Calling*. Jossey-Bass, San Francisco, p.108.

6   See note 2, p.68.

7   From an interview in summer 2002.

8   From an interview in summer 2002.

8

Recognition and Rewards

'You get what you reward.'

I don't know who said that first. Attila the Hun, maybe, as he portioned out the spoils of battle, giving the best to the warriors who fought hardest. Or an ancient pyramid builder, who discovered that if you fed a slave better for doing extra work, he would work hard again the next day. Whatever its origin, it's axiomatic in business today.

Yet it does seem to fly in the face of some of what this book has said so far, because until now the book has been mostly about intrinsic motivation – good feelings that arise from doing the work. The focus for managers has been on providing opportunities for employees to do meaningful work and creating an environment that reinforces the satisfaction that work provides.

So this chapter takes a change in direction. Rewards are extrinsic motivators; they come from outside. The good feeling they give rise to is anticipation of enjoying the expected prize. There is no question that, for most employees, anticipating a reward helps drive performance. There is also no question that having no such expectation can stifle it.

SMART ANSWERS TO
TOUGH QUESTIONS

Q: Which has a bigger impact on performance, extrinsic rewards or intrinsic motivation?

A: It's not a question of either/or. To do their best, most people need both.

This chapter is about the kinds of rewards that supervisors and managers have control over. Many of them are non-monetary ways to recognize employee performance. Some have minor costs that are within the manager's budget and discretion.

The impact of rewards

Recognition and rewards work to energize employees because:

- *They reaffirm the employee's feelings of competence.* As the previous chapter said, most of us feel more confident of our own competence when it's confirmed by an outside source. So an extrinsic motivator can actually bolster our internal motivation.

- *They demonstrate that the organization values the employee.* Just like competence, self-worth needs some reflection from others too. Being recognized by the organization reinforces the pride we feel in our own performance and our own value as a worker and human being.

- *They are, in themselves, desirable.* Rewards can take a lot of forms, from dinners out to days off to prize assignments. Such things have value in themselves. If they know they can earn such rewards, many people will put in extra effort – at least in the short run – to merit them.

- *They demonstrate to employees what the organization considers valuable.* If I work hard and get rewarded for it, that tells me that my employer values hard work. To maintain my employer's respect, I'll continue to work hard. That's the good side. The dark side is that if I associate a reward given to me or someone else with actions like cutting corners to meet a goal, giving short shrift to a customer, or toadying up to management, I'm going to assume the organization values those behaviours. A variation on 'You get what you reward' goes, 'Be careful what you reward, because that's what you'll get.' There's a lesson in an old parable: 'A fisherman felt a bump against the side of his boat. Looking down, he saw a snake with a frog in its mouth. The fisherman grabbed the oar and whacked the snake. It dropped the frog, which swam away quickly. Then feeling sorry for the snake, the fisherman looked around for something to give it. All he had was a bottle of rum, so he gave the snake a long swig. The snake swam off happily. In a few minutes, the fisherman felt another bump. There was the snake again, this time holding two frogs in its mouth.'[1]

Motivating with rewards: some guidelines

People, like water snakes, don't always respond to rewards as expected. But you can use recognition and rewards with maximum impact if you follow these guidelines:

1 Determine what to reward based on organizational values and goals

If those values and goals are worth more than the paper they are written on, then it stands to reason that you'll want to motivate your employees to behave in ways that align with them and contribute to them. Of course, if you work in an organization where there is an obvious disconnect between stated values and the example set by top management, then you'll have to make judicious choices as to which values you want to emphasize. Especially if you've got a bunch of cynics on board – they won't be turned on by the prospect of a reward for behaviour that top management professes but doesn't abide by itself. On the other hand, if you're working with a crew of idealists, they just might be supercharged by the challenge of setting their own example for the rest of the organization.

2 Specify reward criteria

If you want to a reward to motivate employees to perform in a certain way, then you've got to be really clear about what kind of performance will win a reward. If employees understand the criteria, then performing to them and earning a reward is within their control. That's motivating. But if the criteria are left open or defined only by words like 'improved' or 'special' or 'beyond expectations', those employees who hope for a reward and don't get one are going to feel mystified at best and quite likely resentful. Neither one is likely to inspire much desire to keep trying.

If the criteria are unclear, employees will come up with their own reasons why a co-worker earns a reward and they don't. They'll probably assume one of these:

- *Favouritism.* Who's most likely to earn an undefined reward? Probably someone who has gotten close enough to the manager to figure out what the manager wants. To the winner's co-workers, such a reward won't look like a payback for extra effort. It will look like playing favourites.

- *Luck.* If nobody knew how the reward would be decided, employees may assume that anyone who earned it must have lucked out, just happened to have done something that caught the manager's fancy. It's an explanation that won't cause as much resentment as charges of favouritism, but it is likely to inspire some shrugs instead of renewed efforts.

- *The criteria are very narrow.* If their jobs are nothing like those of co-workers who get rewards, employees may assume they have no chance of earning one themselves.

You can avoid such demotivating misconceptions by making the reward criteria very specific and reviewing them with all your employees to help your people recognize how the requirements apply to the work they do.

3 Involve your employees in designing the reward system

If you enlist your employees' input, you not only give them some control over it – and that's an intrinsic motivator – you can also minimize some common difficulties, like the fuzzy criteria mentioned above, that undermine many reward systems. Rewards actually demotivate when:

- Employees don't know what to do to earn them.

- They are not sure what it was for when they do get a reward.

- There's a perception that you've got to ingratiate yourself with management to get rewarded.

- The same people get rewarded over and over.

- Some jobs provide more opportunities for earning rewards than do other jobs.

- People feel they are doing their best and still don't get rewarded.

Involving employees in creating the rewards programme gives them the opportunity and the responsibility to design those complaints out of it. When they establish their own reward criteria, they:

- know what to do to earn a reward;

- know what the rewards mean: if the tangible reward is a mug or a paperweight, it has some value because they know what it stands for;

- respect other people for earning rewards, rather than suspecting favouritism; and

- can broaden the criteria so that everyone, in every job, has an opportunity to be recognized for the work they do.

When you invite employee input into your work unit rewards programme, your responsibility is to set parameters: the organizational values and goals the programme should uphold, your own goals for the programme, the budget, and, if any, the non-negotiables – criteria that are required or disallowed.

4 Reward everyone who meets the criteria

If you want to motivate a few, highly competitive people to ever higher levels of performance, have a contest every month and make a really big deal out of recognizing the winner.

But if you want to motivate all your employees to perform at their very best, forget the competition. Base your reward system on individualized stretch criteria and honour everyone who achieves them.

For most employees and over the long haul, criteria-based rewards are better motivators than competitive-based rewards because there aren't any losers. A competition has one winner (or perhaps two or three) and a bunch of losers who worked hard and gained nothing. How many times does that have to happen before they stop trying? For some people, not many. True, even when the rewards are criteria-based, some people will fail to meet the criteria, and they won't earn a reward. But if they don't, they'll know it was their own fault, not because someone else walked away with the prize. And they'll also know what they have to do differently next time to improve their chances of success.

5 Make sure the reward is worth the effort

Assuming you don't have a budget that lets you toss around large sums of money, the rewards you give out (other than salary increases and organizationally sanctioned bonuses) probably fall into three categories:

- small amounts of cash or the equivalent in prizes like gift certificates or theatre tickets;

- token awards like engraved mugs, paperweights, or plaques; and

• ceremonial recognition of employees' accomplishments.

The first category is nice, but probably not enough, in itself, to inspire major, long-term performance improvement. Ditto the second. In fact, when such items proliferate they may begin to inspire ridicule from the cynics in your midst. The third is great while it lasts, but it's not something you want to do every day, or it would become commonplace and lose impact.

Beyond a brief bout of pleasure, what makes all these rewards worth the effort is that they are symbols of how much the organization, manager and co-workers appreciate and esteem the work of the recipient. For the reward to be motivating, that connection needs to be explicit and reinforced through ongoing confirmation of the individual's value to the organization.

KILLER QUESTIONS

Why would anyone want another mug, plaque, paperweight?

To make that happen, it's a good idea to link the tangible, symbolic reward with a recognition ceremony, preferably one in which top management plays a role. Then make it really worthwhile by enriching the reward winner's job in a way that is interesting and challenging.

6 Upend the golden rule

Smart quotes

'Do not do unto others as you would that they should do unto you. Their tastes may not be the same.'

George Bernard Shaw

Some wise management thinkers have suggested that the biggest problem managers have in motivating people is that they give out rewards they would like to get themselves – golden rule kind of thinking. It works for employees whose preferences, personality and ambitions match those of their managers. But it can fail miserably – to the disappointment of all – when the employee's choices are

'People assume their personality happens to be human nature. In 1908, Freud presented the anal character type – obstinate, super clean, stingy. But when Carl Jung first lectured in Zurich on this, one of the doctors there said, "Why do you call this anal? This is human nature."'

Michael Maccoby[2]

SMART VOICES

distinctly different. So the manager who makes a big public hoop-la over the accomplishments of a shy introvert may just scare the person into lying low the next time a high-profile opportunity comes along. A tireless manager who offers another high-pressure project as a reward for putting in long, stressful hours won't get thanks from an employee who really wants more time with the family. Conversely, getting a week off as a show of appreciation for a job well done is going to feel more like punishment than reward to a workaholic.

Instead of feeling hurt if your efforts to reward people aren't appreciated, tailor your rewards to each individual.

- *Give options.* Tell the people you want to honour that you appreciate their good work and would like to reward them. Then offer a range of suggestions and let them decide.

- *Be a detective.* Pay close attention to your employees. What tasks give them pleasure? What spare time activities do they talk about? When have you heard them say, 'I'd like to do that …?'

- *Check with someone who knows.* If you're planning to honour an employee with an event or a tangible reward, talk to someone who knows the person's preferences: a good friend at work, perhaps, or a partner at home.

When Patti Dowse, president of Erda Leather, Inc. in Cambridge, Maine, was 13, she asked her mother's advice about what to get a friend for her birthday. 'Get her what you would like,' her mother replied. 'She'll like that too.' That worked fine, so ...

'On my mother's next birthday, I got her the sound track from the movie Ben Hur, which I had just seen and loved. I remember her quizzical look, and that I found it in her give-away box shortly after. A lesson learned. All people are not the same.

'At work, I try to recognize that each individual has different wants and needs, so rewards need to reflect that. I want to treat everyone as equal, but not as if they were the same. Some want more money, while others want more time off, more freedom in their hours, a tape player to listen to while working. As money is often in short supply, I find I can often create a good feeling by rewarding with recognition, or by providing something that doesn't cost too much.

'All my workers love to be taken out to lunch, so we do that often. They like to have tea or coffee, so I have just arranged for a water cooler/heater, so they won't forget their hot water in the microwave so often! As individuals, I have given them the reward points from our phone company (which one woman used to get a very fancy Christmas gift for her husband, something she could not have bought herself), days or afternoons off, items from our stock of handmade things, items that I trade for at wholesale craft events. I always try to find out if these things are appreciated, so I don't waste the effort.'[3]

- *Go ahead and ask the person:* 'Here's what I'd like to do to recognize your achievement ... Would you be comfortable with that or is there something else you'd prefer?

- *Don't do anything that could embarrass the person:* Unless you know the person well, no jokes, no roasts, no calls for a speech.

- *Don't make assumptions about the person's commitment and gratitude:* Perhaps you didn't get the enthusiastic response you hoped for. It doesn't diminish the fact that the individual did a good job and is capable of doing more.

7 Reward behaviours as well as outcomes

If you are a manager, there's a good chance you've rewarded someone lately with an award, a celebration or some positive feedback. What was that reward for? My guess is it was for producing a desired result: processing X number of cases, building Y number of widgets, answering Z number of calls. Most rewards focus on outcomes. There's a lot to be said for that. After all, organizations thrive on results.

But there's also a lot to be said for recognizing and rewarding desirable behaviours. As recent high-profile corporate calamities confirm, results aren't all that count. Behaviours matter too, and exemplary behaviour also deserves to be rewarded. In fact, by rewarding behaviour, you can accomplish positive changes that might never occur if you waited for an outcome. By rewarding positive behaviours, you can:

- sustain enthusiasm for a lengthy project when the result is a long way down the road;

- recognize employees for good efforts if a project gets cancelled or fails due to circumstances outside their control; and

- reinforce small behaviour changes by employees who have been performing unsatisfactorily – over time, these changes can add up to an outcome worth celebrating.

KILLER QUESTIONS

Where's the dividing line between motivation and manipulation?

Some people think there's a danger in rewarding behaviours, fearing that it's a covert form of control. This poses the question, perhaps, of where motivation turns into manipulation. If you give a small gift to an employee who works through lunch one day, is that manipulation? Perhaps, if you are hoping the person will do it every day. But not if it was a one-time event to whittle away at a backlog. If you praise someone for correcting mistakes without being told, is that manipulation? Hardly. That's just good management. If you thank a chronic latecomer sincerely for coming to work on time one morning, is that manipulation? Not unless it's manipulative to reinforce appropriate behaviour. And if you reward people for being creative and trying new things, that's encouraging them to take more control of their work, not less.

8 Say 'thank you' frequently

If there's one reward that's always available to give, it's a simple, sincere 'thank you'. It's free, it's in unlimited supply, and it's a suitable reward for employees, co-workers and even your boss. And yet, I've heard people remark scornfully: 'What? I'm supposed to thank people just for doing their jobs?'

Well yes, why not? We thank people for passing the bread at the dinner table. We teach our kids to write thank-you notes even for gifts they don't like. Then they grow up and go to work, and the words seem to disappear from the language. Over and over, I hear workers say, 'What's the point of going an extra mile around here? Nobody even says thank you.' What kind of a message does that give people? That their work is less important than a slice of bread. That's not very motivating.

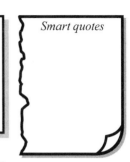

Smart quotes

'They have time to punish the worker whose sloppiness costs the plant 37 minutes of downtime. They have time to tack up an "Employee of the Week" award to thank the number one worker who really stands out. But that leaves a huge number of people in between, people who are neither "eagles" nor slackers ... those people need reinforcement, too.'

Fran Tarkenton and Tad Tuleja, *How To Motivate People*[4]

You may even have heard employees scoff, 'I don't want to be thanked.' They too buy into the prevailing attitude. But I bet you've never heard someone say, 'I don't want positive feedback.' And a well-phrased thank-you is positive feedback of the best kind.

To be really effective, a thank-you should be specific and descriptive. 'Thanks, folks, for a great job' tossed over your shoulder on the way out the door doesn't mean much. In fact, it might leave the recipients wondering if you really even know what they did. The best thank-you messages:

- describe exactly what the person did that you appreciate; and

- tell why it was important.

Here's an example: 'Thanks for pitching in to eliminate the backlog. Your efforts went beyond the call of duty, but because of them we're on track now to meet our quarterly goals, and, better yet, you've made hundreds of customers happy.'

There's an auxiliary benefit to saying 'thank you' that seldom gets mentioned. It feels good on both sides. It's as uplifting to the thanker as it is to the person being thanked. In fact, it's contagious. The more often you say it, the more often others will too – and everybody's motivation gets a boost.

Recognizing both superstars and poor performers

Everybody needs recognition, and few people feel they get enough of it. In fact, companies that do exit interviews often discover that not getting the recognition they feel they deserve is one reason people leave.

If anyone were to get adequate recognition, you would expect it to be stellar performers. Yet they often feel as neglected as everyone else. Too often, managers take them for granted and fail to acknowledge their consistently superior efforts until it's too late and a superstar's performance starts to slip or a fast-tracker makes tracks right out the door.

So along with the appropriate compensation that your top performers hopefully are getting, be generous with your thanks and make sure their accomplishments are recognized by top management too.

KILLER QUESTIONS

How can I use recognition to motivate someone whose performance is too poor to warrant a reward?

The people it's hardest to reward are your poor performers. Yet they're probably the ones you most need to motivate. To begin with, focus on the final two guidelines above: reward behaviours and say 'thank you'. Recognize small improvements and positive changes even if performance results aren't yet up to snuff. You're not going to nominate the person for employee of the year, but you can certainly say: 'Thank you for getting the draft to me on time. I'll be able to give it the full attention it deserves.'

Be very specific so the person knows exactly what she's done right. If it boosts her self-esteem a little, she might get to like your feedback so much she'll look for other ways to earn it. And eventually those incremental behavioural changes can add up to a significant change in performance.

The smartest things in this chapter

- Receiving a reward reaffirms a employee's feelings of competence, demonstrates that the organization values the employee, and reveals what the organization considers valuable.

- When employees help design reward systems, they know how to earn a reward and why others get rewarded.

- Symbolic rewards can be meaningful if they are reinforced through ongoing confirmation of the employee's value to the organization.

- Reward people by giving them what they want, not what you'd like.

- Say 'thank you' frequently.

- Poor performers don't get much positive feedback, so for them, recognize even small improvements.

Notes

1   Adapted from a tale retold by Michael LeBoeuf in (1985) *The Greatest Management Principle in the World*. Putnam, New York.

2   From an interview, spring 2002.

3   From personal correspondence, summer 2002.

4   Tarkenton, F. & T. Tuleja (1986) *How To Motivate People*. HarperCollins, New York, p.20.

9

Rewarding Relationships

If you haven't said any of these yourself, I'll bet you've heard other managers say them:

- 'We're here to get a job done, not to make friends.'

- 'They don't have to like me; they just have to respect me.'

- 'This isn't a social club.'

All of them suggest that work would improve if we could just eliminate social interaction from the workplace.

Not so. In fact, for many people, the opportunity to interact with others and to build meaningful relationships is what keeps them coming to work every day. And although working from home is growing in popularity, many people who do so stay actively in touch with their manager and colleagues

'Where is the marketplace where one can exchange a lifelong friendship for a monetary sum?'

Paul Lawrence and Nitin Nohria, *Driven*[1]

by e-mail and phone as much to feel connected and cared about as to resolve work needs.

Motivation researchers all recognize the human need for relationships at work. Maslow put belongingness and love right in the middle of his hierarchy of needs. Herzberg lists relationships with manager, peers and subordinates as hygiene factors, whose absence guarantees job dissatisfaction. Another motivational psychologist, David McClelland, proposed a theory of only three primary needs, one of which is affiliation (the other two are power and achievement). Maccoby includes relationships in his 4 Rs of motivation (see Chapter 3), and Katzenbach asserts that belonging is a generic fulfilment need.

If you are a manager, nobody suggests you should strive to become best buddies with the people who report to you. But they'll be more enthusiastic about working for you and feel more confident about tackling new projects if you develop trusting and caring relationships with them and create an atmosphere that encourages them to bond with each other in work affiliations and friendship.

Manager/employee relationships that energize

Energizing manager/employee relationships are built on trust, caring, mutual appreciation, two-way respect and ongoing communication.

Trust

Trust is the very foundation of any successful relationship. Any liaison that is not grounded in two-way trust is wary at best, self-serving and potentially subversive.

You earn trust by:

- *Behaving reliably.* Share your values and act in accordance with them consistently.

- *Keeping your word.* Before you commit to doing something, make sure that it's within your power.

- *Keeping confidences.* As you build relationships, people will tell you things not intended for the ears of the world. Be absolutely close-mouthed about the private affairs of others.

- *Treating people fairly.* You can't treat everyone exactly the same, but you can treat them all by the same set of standards.

- *Sharing information.* Pass on all the information you get that is relevant to their jobs.

- *Standing up for them* in disputes with others outside your unit.

- *Treating mistakes as opportunities to learn,* rather than punishable of-fences. Freedom from fear goes a long way toward building trust.

- *Trusting others.* Trust is a two-way street. To earn it, you have to extend it to others. That calls for entrusting people with some personal informa-tion about you as well as encouraging them to make and implement their own work decisions.

In their book, *The New Why Teams Don't Work*, Harvey Robbins and Michael Finley, offer leaders these strategies for building trust:[2]

1 'Have clear, consistent goals.'

2 'Be open, fair and willing to listen.'

3 'Be decisive.'

4 'Support all other team members.'

5 'Take responsibility for team actions.'

6 'Give credit to team members.'

7 'Be sensitive to the needs of team members.'

8 'Respect the opinions of others.'

9 'Empower team members to act.'

Caring

At the heart of any healthy relationship is genuinely caring about the other person. How much you care reveals itself to you when you feel sincere joy in another's happiness, accomplishments and good fortune, both on and off the job, and experience sorrow over the individual's misfortunes and crises, both personal and professional. You express how much you care to other people when you acknowledge their special times, celebrate their highlights with them and support them in times of difficulty. To be able to do those things, you have to put some time and effort into getting to know them personally, as well as uncovering their professional hopes, fears and satisfactions.

To talk about a 'set of how-tos' or a 'recipe for caring' would subvert it from a genuine emotion to a mere outward show, which everyone would see through pretty quickly. But there are actions that make it likely for genuine caring to blossom, and when you do care, there are behaviours that demonstrate that to others.

- *Practice self-disclosure.* Find time for personal conversations – what you did over the weekend, favourite books, movies you enjoyed, volunteer activities, your kids' latest shenanigans. The more you are willing to share, the more the other person will open up. Work your way up to revealing hopes and dreams for the future. Broached carefully, it can even help to share some disappointments and concerns, especially if doing so demonstrates your empathy around issues the other person is struggling with.

- *Notice how people express their individuality* – the artwork they display, the family photos, the pictures of vacations and pets, even the clothes they wear. Every picture has a story; invite people to share those stories with you. Be interested, and be very careful not to be judgmental.

- *Mark personal and professional milestones.* Birthday cards are practically de rigueur; a birthday breakfast – even coffee and a doughnut shared over a desk – might be even better. Other good card opportunities include: new homes, children's school achievements, engagements, anniversaries, even new cars. Arrange a celebration when an employee completes an educational programme, finishes a project or earns a coveted role in an interdepartmental project.

- *Show your appreciation.* Small gifts and favours are appropriate when someone does something special. But a sincere 'thank you' is best. This is a reminder worth repeating. Thank your employees for any action that helped you personally, that went beyond the call of duty, that was out of the ordinary for them, and even for doing their everyday jobs.

- *Be sensitive to personal crises.* A worst-case example was the story a lower Manhattan worker told the *New York Times* about being wakened early in the morning on 12 September 2001 by a call from her employer demanding that she get to work right then for a meeting. People need time and support to deal with issues less overwhelming than major terrorist attacks. Illnesses – their own and those of people close to them – troubled children, financial problems; all of these may weigh heavily on an employee and require days off, shortened work hours, empathetic listening and sensitivity to heightened emotions at work.

Respect

There's a lot to be said for one of this chapter's opening statements: 'They don't have to like me; they just have to respect me.' Indeed, respect is more crucial to a productive business relationship than is liking (just don't confuse liking people with caring about them). It may be hard to 'like' someone who – by our taste – is too jovial or too serious, talks too much or is too quiet, is too prurient or too prudish, even too ambitious or too laid back. But none of those things matter much in a business relationship, and most people recognize that.

The problem with the 'don't like me, just respect me' attitude is that it sometimes implies an interpretation of respect that is a poor substitute for the real thing. Respect used this way is often a euphemism for deference. What it's really saying is 'Acknowledge my superior position, defer to my power, avoid my retribution.' That's not respect, that's fear, and while it might have a short-range motivational impact, it's poisonous in the long term.

> To earn respect, you could do worse than to follow the advice in Rudyard Kipling's poem, *If*:
>
> 'If you can keep your head when all about you
> Are losing theirs and blaming it on you;
> If you can trust yourself when all men doubt you,
> But make allowance for their doubting too;
> If you can wait and not be tired by waiting,
> Or, being lied about, don't deal in lies,
> Or, being hated, don't give way to hating,
> And yet don't look too good, nor talk too wise;'

Smart quotes

You'll earn genuine respect, not fear, if you:

- *Stand up for what you believe in.* Taking a stand for what's right when you see injustices in your organization may be risky behaviour, but it will earn you respect, even from those who disagree with you.

- *Are open to your employees' opposing points of view.* Does this contradict the point above? Not really. Being willing to defend your own beliefs doesn't require rigidity and unwillingness to adapt to a better idea.

- *Redouble your efforts around all the points above under trust.* Respect without trust is an oxymoron.

- *Show respect for others.* Listening well is key here, especially listening without passing judgement. (There is more about listening under 'Communication' below.) Accepting others' decisions shows respect, too. So does welcoming feedback on your behaviour from others. Building a relationship depends upon respecting both the professional skills and the lifestyles of others. You could turn around the statement we started with to make it apply here: you don't have to like your employees, but you do have to respect them.

'To improve interpersonal communication, managers should focus on relationship skills that consist of the following:

- Attentiveness

- Empathy

- Genuineness

- Nonverbal techniques

- Rapport

- Understanding'

Jerry W Gilley, Nathaniel Boughton, Ann Maycunich, *The Performance Challenge*[3]

Communication

When it comes right down to it, building relationships is all about communication. Communicating well isn't just about delivery; it takes a combination of both listening and presenting skills.

- *Listening.* Some people are born good listeners, but with practice anyone can learn the skills.
  - *Pay attention to the speaker.* Do it visibly: lean forward a little; make adequate (not constant) eye contact; reflect the person's emotions with your facial expressions. Do it audibly: speak enough sounds and phrases, such as 'Uh huh' and 'I see', to prove you are still awake.
  - *Acknowledge the speaker's statements and feelings.* Paraphrase often. Put the person's statement into your own words and feed them back.

When you do that, the speaker will reply, 'That's right,' or 'That's not what I meant.' Either way, you're on the road to better understanding. In addition, reflect the person's feelings with responses like, 'I understand that you are worried.' Paraphrasing and reflecting are practically magic. They let you express honest empathy even if you don't agree with what the person is saying.

- *Ask questions to clarify.* Asking just enough questions shows your interest; asking too many begins to feel like an interrogation.
- *Avoid arguing – at least, not yet.* Even if you disagree with the speaker, you won't hear the facts if you react before getting the whole story.
- *Recap and confirm.* When you are satisfied you have all the pertinent information, recap it in a few sentences. It's helpful to begin with a phrase like 'Let me sum up what you've said. What happened is ....
You are concerned that ....' This is paraphrasing and reflecting again, but this time you cover everything. Then confirm your understanding with a question like, 'Did I describe that correctly?' When the answer is 'Yes', you've listened actively, empathetically, respectfully and without passing judgement.

- *Presenting.* This covers conveying information, delivering news or expressing your point of view. Even asking for help or making an assignment is a form of presenting, since a crucial part of that communication is explaining the need. Skilful presenters reinforce relationships by expressing themselves in a way that is:
  - *Clear.* Clarity is in the ears and brain of the listener, not the words of the presenter. Part of your role as a presenter is to encourage your listener to practice all the active listening techniques above. Ostensibly, that's why most presentations end with 'Any questions?' But by that time your listeners may well have forgotten the questions that raced through their minds earlier, may have forgotten half of what you said earlier, and might have been thinking about their next meeting or what

to have for dinner that night. The best way to ensure clarity is to make your presentation interactive throughout. If your listeners don't cut in with questions, then punctuate your statements periodically by asking 'What's your reaction to that?', 'How do you think that will affect you?' or 'Do you have ideas for how to deal with that?' You can even encourage paraphrasing by asking: 'Would you mind telling me what you understood by that? I want to be sure I expressed it clearly.'

By involving the listener, the presenter not only improves the chances that the listener receives the message as intended, but also impresses on him the importance of the message and reinforces the relationship between them ('we're in this together' is the implication).

- *Complete.* When it comes to what managers expect their employees to tell them, the most common catchphrase is: 'Don't surprise me.' Yet management surprises employees all time with new information that blows away everything they've been working on. It used to be acceptable for managers to feed their employees information on a need-to-know basis. Perhaps that hasn't changed; what has changed is the assessment of how much employees need to know. The new answer to that is everything the manager can learn that has a bearing on employees' work now and might have in the future.
- *Timely.* Anyone who has been on the receiving end of a less-than-excellent annual performance review knows first hand the importance of timely communication. 'What can I do with this information now?' the employee wonders, listening to the reasons for an unexpected 'satisfactory' (if not lower) rating. 'If I'd known earlier, I could have done something about it.' The uselessness of such feedback is one reason why many organizations are replacing once-sacred annual reviews with much more frequent feedback. Individual performance feedback has a limited shelf-life, as does organization and unit-wide performance data, company plans and expectations, market-place and competitor news, and all the other information that shapes the way people approach their jobs.

- *Adapted to the needs of the receiver.* After a plant-wide series of interviews and focus groups, I once delivered feedback to a plant manager, revealing that most employees felt in the dark about company and plant plans and performance. He stared at me, amazed. 'But you know I give them that information,' he exclaimed. 'You were there.' And he was right. That morning I had attended one of his quarterly all-hands meetings and heard his detailed presentation on company results versus goals. Obviously there was a disconnect. But why? The forum maybe. It was a long meeting of a large group in a big room. The team at the table where I sat already knew they hadn't met their team goals that quarter, thanks to some mechanical problems, and they pretty much tuned out, talking quietly among themselves throughout. Perhaps smaller meetings with each team, with more give and take, would have been more effective. Sometimes you just have to keep trying until you find a process that works.

Smart things to say about motivation

The purpose of speaking is not to make noise. It's to be understood.

Overcoming rigid hierarchies, paternalism, maternalism

If you want the people who report to you to think for themselves, contribute original ideas, solve problems, and set and pursue challenging goals, then you'll want to avoid some traditional manager/employee relationships. The first can be characterized by, 'I'm the boss, so do as I say.' That nips initiative in the bud. The second is the paternalistic, 'I know what's best, and I'll take care of you.' That's comforting but stifling. The third is the maternalistic, 'Here, let me do that for you.' That kind of relationship is smothering.

Smart quotes

'People will sit up and take notice of you if you sit up and take notice of what makes them sit up and take notice.'

Harvey A. Robbins, *How To Speak and Listen Effectively*[4]

SMART VOICES

'Employees come to work for two reasons: first, to do a good job and to contribute to the organization and, second, to be with their coworkers, their friends. And, by the way, these are the same reasons I come to work.'

Horst Schulze, former CEO, Ritz-Carlton Hotels[5]

Co-worker connections

For many people, relationships with co-workers are what make going to work more than just a way to put food on the table. They turn a workplace into a friendly, supportive, self-affirming space, a place where people go an extra mile to help each other and because they can count on help from each other. As a manager, you can build on those positives by implementing co-operative processes and creating an environment that encourages employees to bond with each other.

- *Maximize opportunities to cooperate.* Form teams, where people depend upon each other to achieve a common goal. Encourage employees to enlist each other's help in solving problems. Reward employees both for asking for and giving help to each other. Promote on-the-job cross-training and mentor/mentee relationships between veterans and newcomers.

- *Minimize reasons to compete.* Avoid contests or job assignments that pit co-workers against each other.

- *Validate healthy socializing.* When you see people socializing, think of it as relationship-building, not slacking off. The time they spend getting to know and trust each other can lead to productive co-operation on projects and tasks. (If you think it's really gone too far, here's a technique a lot of managers use. Join in for a while, amiably and with no sign of disapproval. When you leave, the group will probably break up.) Take the whole group to lunch now and then and don't bring up work topics.

About that social club

In fact, in their own way, many workplaces are social clubs, and that's as it should be. Humans are social creatures. They value families, join organizations, build communities, seeking and thriving on connections with each other. It's only natural that they will flourish and grow when work provides the same kind of connections.

The smartest things in this chapter

- Healthy manager–employee relationships are built on trust, caring, mutual appreciation, two-way respect and ongoing communications.

- Listening actively is as important – if not more important – to good communications as is presenting convincingly.

- Rigid hierarchies, paternalism ('I'll take care of you') and maternalism ('I'll do that for you') encourage employee dependence rather than initiative.

- For some people, co-worker friendships are what lure them to work every day.

Notes

1   Lawrence, P.R. & N. Nohria (2002) *Driven*. Jossey-Bass, San Francisco, p.77.

2   Robbins, H. & M. Finley (2000) *The New Why Teams Don't Work*. Berrett-Koehler, San Francisco, pp. 161–67.

3   Gilley, J.W., N.W. Boughton & A. Maycunich (1999) *The Performance Challenge*. Perseus, Cambridge, MA, p.57.

4   Robbin, H.A. (1992) *How To Speak and Listen Effectively*. AMACOM, New York, p.17.

5   Quoted in Goman, C.K. (1998) *This Isn't the Company I Joined*. Wiley, New York, p.42.

Part III
A More Motivating Workplace

The focus of the book shifts now, from the one-on-one relationship between manager and employee to an organization-wide perspective. The next chapters look at organizational characteristics, policies and practices that inspire or restrain employee energy and commitment. But the point of view is still that of managers, whose role it is to interpret top management's decisions and actions at the work unit level.

Chapter 10 is all about money, looking at both its positive and negative motivational impacts.

Chapter 11 concentrates on vision and leadership, two characteristics that differentiate between high- and low-energy organizations.

Chapter 12 focuses on teams, whose proliferation is a hallmark of this era, and which have the potential to provide employees with exciting opportunities and supportive relationships.

Chapter 13 looks at how the economic downturn and companies' penchant for repeated reorganizations and lay-offs affect employee motivation. It examines what managers can do to support employees in tough times and even whet their appetite for the challenges change brings.

10

Money: The Gorilla in the Middle of the Book

It hasn't been easy to write a little more than half of this book and barely mention money. It's been hovering like the proverbial 800-pound gorilla in the middle of the table. Ignoring it has been hard work.

Now, as the theme of the book shifts to an organizational perspective on motivation, the gorilla demands to be heard. Compensation is usually an organization-wide issue, and it's often the one that pops up first when people are asked what they like or don't like about the enterprise they work for.

So it's time to confront the question, 'Is money a motivator?' If we limit the definition of motivation to internal drives, then the answer must be no. But as a practical matter, for anyone more concerned with generating performance than with psychological correctness, the more important question is probably, 'Does money (or

> *Smart quotes*
>
> 'There is nothing in the world so demoralizing as money.'
>
> Sophocles, *Antigone*

its pursuit) energize workers and propel them to superior performance?' As the accompanying quotes show, the argument between the opposing responses has been going on for millennia. This chapter will examine both sides.

The case for yes

When you read about the amounts of money that corporations pay to lure high-profile executives into their top slots, it's pretty hard to argue that money isn't a motivator. No company would pay all that money to someone who said, 'Oh don't worry about salary or bonuses or stock options. I don't care if they're meagre. It's just the challenge that interests me.'

Nor is it just in the upper echelons that money talks. How often have you heard employees mutter, 'Just give me the dough' in discussions that are supposed to be about job enrichment or perks or non-monetary benefits?

A few years ago the owner of a small factory in New England had an unexpectedly prosperous year. In possession of an unanticipated profit, she called a meeting of all employees to decide what to do with it. She explained how this windfall had occurred and invited their input into its disposition, suggesting some options. One alternative was to divide it among everyone as bonuses. Another was to get a new air-conditioning system for the plant, and the other choices were also in this vein, geared toward increasing everyone's on-the-job comfort.

The owner, hoping to promote a sense of ownership among employees, was surprised and dismayed at the reactions of some workers. Far from seeing the occasion as an opportunity to have a say in company policy, they protested that the owner was asking them to foot the bill for plant maintenance. They wanted the money, which they claimed as rightfully theirs. As they saw it, air-conditioning the building was the owner's responsibility and should be done at no cost to them. Somehow, just raising the possibility of bonuses as one option had made that money theirs.

Why money works

Money influences on-the-job behaviour for two reasons, because of what it can buy and because of what it symbolizes.

What money can buy

Around the world, millions of people toil at jobs that offer little intrinsic reward, but that allow them to meet their basic needs for a roof over the head and food on the table. At its most elementary level, money buys rudimentary security; Maslow recognized that as a human need and Herzberg placed it among his hygiene factors – things we need to ward off dissatisfaction. For anyone unlucky enough not to be born with a silver spoon, working is the acceptable way of obtaining money.

Of course, most of us want more – and the more we get, the more we want – nicer home, furniture, clothes, cars, vacations, better schools for our children. There's always something that costs just a little more than we can afford until we get a promotion, a bonus or a better paying job elsewhere. Luckily for the sake of the lower-paid but essential 'helping' professions like teaching and social work, some people are satisfied with fewer of the tangible things money can buy and willing to sacrifice for the intangible satisfaction of helping others. But there are many other people who choose their fields of work partly on the basis of their potential earnings – or potential buying power. For those people, every career move is influenced by the money associated with it.

The lifestyle we want and the money required to support it affect our choice of profession, decision to take a specific job, decision to leave it for another job, and sometimes our willingness to work at tasks we find unpleasant. But what money can buy is only one of its sources of power, and often not even the dominant one. The other reason money has such an impact is that we use it to measure a number of important intangibles.

What money symbolizes

Many people read money like tea leaves. It reveals to them how important they are to the organization for which they work, how they rank in relation to their co-workers, their standing in the community and, in rarefied circles, their prestige in the world. It measures for them the worth of their own achievements.

Worth to the organization

At its most obvious level, a fat pay increase tells an employee, 'We think highly of you and have plans for you in this organization.' A meagre one says, 'We don't think you are anything special.' To anyone who is really listening, no increase at all says, 'We don't really want you here, but we can't come up with a good enough reason to fire you.'

Smart quotes

'Money is how you keep score.'

H. Wayne Huizenga, former chairman of Blockbuster Entertainment Corporation and said to be one of the richest men in America[1]

Of course, there are all sorts of circumstances that affect what organizations pay. A skimpy increase might mean the salary increase budget is tight this year and the manager is doling it out equally. No increase might mean a budget freeze. But in those circumstances, money tells another story, one that is often interpreted by employees as an organization in trouble, led by ineffectual upper management. And these days, it may also be read as greedy management, skimming off the top while mistreating employees. These interpretations aren't likely to inspire commitment and willingness to work extra hard.

In a union shop, where pay increases are determined more by contract than by performance assessment, employees may not make a connection between an increase and their own value to the organization. But they may see increases as indicative of what management thinks of labour as a whole, and that can influence their commitment to the enterprise and willingness to perform.

Ranking

When two or more people have the same job in an organization and their salaries are different, a mental rank ordering occurs: 'They [the ubiquitous managerial 'they'] like Pat more than me, but at least they regard me higher than Sandy.' What's the impact on motivation? That depends. For some, the thought process might be: 'I want to be at least on Pat's level. Now, what do I have to do to get there?' But for others, the response is: 'After all I've done, they're still paying Pat more. I'm not going to knock myself out any more.'

If it's obvious that the salary ranking is based on seniority, that eliminates the 'Why do they like Pat more than me?' agony. But it can fire another kind of resentment if the more senior person is less skilled and less productive. The opposite problem occurs when organizations hire new people at higher salaries than those of existing employees. Doing so may be necessary to compete in the recruitment market, but to the veterans it says: 'This company doesn't value commitment and loyalty' and, as night follows day, the next thought is: 'So why should I?'

If you think salaries are secret in your organization, don't count on it. They are often the most open secrets in the enterprise. People with access to the numbers let them slip. Or one employee, naively assuming her salary is the same as everyone else's, mentions it: 'Yeah and they expect us to do all that

Smart quotes

'Money is like a mirror to our culture. What we see tells us who we are.'

Jack Needleman, philosopher[2]

for ....' A newly hired person tells his new co-workers how happy he was to get a substantial increase over the .... he earned in his old job. A curious employee makes an anonymous call to Human Resources to find out what the company is offering to fill an open slot. Once, when I was in an internal training department for a large company, I needed to know all executives and managers' grade levels to slot them into training programmes. The information I was given included their salaries, too. It was fascinating reading.

Station in life

All those wonderful things that money can buy are not just toys or possessions to be cherished for their own sake. They are status symbols. The house we live in, the car we drive, our subscriptions to concerts and sporting events, our vacation destinations – all these tell the world we've made it. Or not. Being able to afford prestigious trappings garners us the right introductions, the right invitations and the respect or envy of our neighbours. Money allows us to keep us with the Joneses. Enough of it allows us to be the Joneses.

What will people do to acquire the money that buys them security, perhaps luxury, and tangible proof that they are valued and successful? Most organizations base their compensation programmes on the assumption that people will work hard for it, and for the implied promise of still more money, they will work even harder and contribute more.

Is money a motivator: the case for no

Everyone agrees that money can influence someone's decision to take a job, especially if the person is having a hard time landing a position and

'For most managers, motivating with money confronts two obstacles. The first is their limited control over financial rewards for their employees. The second is that money's success as a motivator is erratic at best.'[3]

the bills are piling up or – at the opposite end of the spectrum – the person has several offers of equal intrinsic appeal. Money may also influence a person's decision to leave a job for a new one. But in between, for keeping an employee consistently energized and productive – that's where relying on money has its limitations.

Short-lived impact

Think of your last pay increase. That day you saw it in your pay cheque – assuming it satisfied you – you felt downright warm and cosy about your relationship with your employer and absolutely gung-ho, ready to take on a new challenge for the organization. That day. But what about a few months later? By that time, you were quite used to it. It had been a while since you'd cashed your cheque, thinking about what you could do with the extra money. In fact, there wasn't any extra money. You'd absorbed it into your regular spending habits. If you were still gung-ho about your job, it wasn't as a result of that pay increase. That's the first shortcoming of money as a motivator. It might inspire a brief burst of grateful activity, but its impact is very short-lived

The entitlement factor

As the years go by, even the brief spurt of appreciation and energy a good pay increase used to generate dims somewhat. That old 'Yes!' that a bigger pay cheque once inspired fades into more of a sigh of relief. That's because what used to feel like a reward evolves into an entitlement. If we get an increase every year, we come to take it for granted, probably even plan our future spending based upon it. Bonuses work the same. The first one or two are godsends, but eventually they too become entitlements. While they may not have much motivating power any more, they most certainly have an impact in their absence. Just as Herzberg said, not getting the expected increase or bonus triggers big dissatisfaction.

Never enough

If you manage other people, there is one thing about money you know for sure. There is never enough of it in your budget to make everybody happy. And reflecting on its short-term impact, you realize there probably isn't enough to keep anybody motivated by money alone. Unlike intrinsic motivators, money always comes out of a limited supply. Oh, you may be able to squeeze out a little more here and there, but it never seeds itself the way excitement over the work can do.

Kills the fun

In some of his experiments on motivation, the psychologist Edward Deci found that paying people for doing a task stripped all the enjoyment out of it for his subjects. Those he didn't pay for doing puzzles went right on doing them after their agreed upon time period ended. Those he paid took their money and left. Of course, not even Deci suggests you'll have more luck hiring and retaining high performers if you don't pay them. Real life and experiments aren't quite the same. But the lesson is that you should probably not expect the same dedication from people who are doing their jobs only for the money that you'll get from people who love their work and get satisfaction out of being a part of your organization.

Making the most of the budget you've got

Money won't make employees love their work, but administered fairly, it can keep smouldering resentment from poisoning their attitude toward their managers, their jobs and the enterprise. At least in the short term, it can generate real enthusiasm among workers who seek their pleasures in costly off-the-job pursuits. And it can affect the self-esteem of employees who read into it how much the organization and the community values them.

If you are a manager, you can make the most of the money you have discretion over if you:

- Match annual pay increases to performance reviews. It's demotivating to get a really good review and an 'average' increase. (Guess which one the employee thinks is the true indicator of the organization's regard.)

- Let employees know what they have to do to earn an above-average increase. Then pay them for it when they succeed. If all your employees are meeting the requirements, you've set the stakes too low. Tell them, 'In this department the average performance is of high quality. To pay a higher increase, I have to raise the bar.'

- If your organization offers annual bonuses or incentive pay, provide regular feedback year round to keep your employees on track toward pre-determined goals.

- Use small cash prizes to reward people when you catch them doing something right. Let them know in advance: 'I'll pay XX amount for achievements like ....' Make sure you are rewarding behaviours and outcomes that everyone has an opportunity to demonstrate. The real cake is the recognition. The cash is icing, so it doesn't have to be big to be meaningful.

- Bear in mind that you may win a bidding war for talent with an offer of more money, and you may retain someone who is thinking of leaving the same way, but it takes more than money to keep people excited by their work and committed to the organization. That's where intrinsic motivation rules.

The smartest things in this chapter

- People work to earn money to satisfy their need for basic financial security and to achieve some degree of luxury.

- Failure to receive enough money to satisfy those needs causes dissatisfaction, which may be reflected in lower performance at work or trigger a search for a new job.

- People use money as a scorecard to judge how the organization values them and how it ranks them in relation to others.

- Financial rewards may inspire short-term performance changes, but over time the additional money is perceived as an entitlement.

Notes

1 Quoted in *The New York Times*, 5 December 1993.

2 Quoted in 'Money and the Meaning of Life' in *Fast Company*, June 1997.

3   Deeprose, D. (1994) *How to Recognize and Reward Employees*. AMA-
    COM, New York, p.11.

11

Organizations That Energize

Why is it that when you walk into some workplaces the air fairly crackles with energy, while in others the atmosphere is so sluggish that the chief activity is the ticking of the clock?

The answer can be summed up in two words: *vision* and *leadership*.

A compelling vision is a call to action. Effective leadership directs and nurtures the action, sustaining it over the long haul.

> *Smart quotes*
>
> 'Where there is no vision, the people perish.'
>
> The Bible, Proverbs 29:18

In the grip of an enthralling future

Someone once said that it's not what we have that motivates us, it's what we want. You could explain a vision then as a big, shared want. Author Burt

Smart quotes

'There is no more powerful engine driving an organization toward excellence and long-range success than an attractive, worthwhile, and achievable vision of the future, widely shared.'

Burt Nanus, *Visionary Leadership*[1]

Nanus describes it more precisely as 'a realistic, credible, attractive future for your organization.'[2] This powerful idea, he says, unleashes some equally powerful forces. The right vision:

- *'Attracts commitment and energizes people'*.[3] Vision makes the difference between working for the money and working for the joy of meeting a worthwhile challenge. Vision is why volunteers flock to charismatic religious or political leaders. It's also why scientists dedicate themselves to projects like mapping the human genome, why engineers push to perfect artificial intelligence, why employees at Southwest Airlines perform ever more extraordinary feats of customer service. People enthusiastically dedicate themselves to the pursuit of a better future – whether spiritual, medical, technological or a matter of comfort and convenience.

- *'Creates meaning in workers' lives'*. Vision is the difference between the proverbial stonecutter who describes his job as chopping up stones and the one who describes it as building a cathedral. It's also the difference between tapping out code for a living and building a high-speed link among people worldwide. Between selling cheap furniture and bringing good design to people of moderate means. Or between processing insurance claims and creating a better future for people devastated by tragedy. Vision turns mundane tasks into important contributions to a worthwhile outcome.

- *'Establishes a standard of excellence'*. Are we doing the right thing and are we doing it right? For organizations with a powerful vision, the answer lies in the evidence that it is moving forward toward the image of its desired future. With a positive answer, people press on. With a negative answer, they regroup, rethink and start again. Without an answer, they simply flounder.

- *'Bridges the present and future'*. The present is a tyrant, constantly demanding that we answer this complaint, fix this problem, respond to this letter or call – right now, sometimes dragging us into a stultifying morass. A strong vision challenges the tyrant. It encourages us to assess the value of those pressing tasks in light of the future and to decide which to strengthen, which to cut or change and what new ones to focus on. It's a lot more fun for employees to get up and go to jobs where their work is moving them toward a desired future outcome than to go put out fires and maintain some status quo.

Whose vision is it?

We read about the importance of a shared vision, but that doesn't mean employees all expect to contribute to defining a vision for the organization. That's the privilege and responsibility of leaders. It's also their responsibility to communicate it relentlessly throughout the organization so that people at all levels understand not only the direction in which the organization is moving, but also how their jobs fuel that forward movement.

The impact of leaders

Defining a compelling vision is just one way that leaders in an enterprise affect employees' commitment to the organization and enthusiasm for their work. Just as important is the degree to which they:

- *Demonstrate high ethical standards* that inspire trust and respect for themselves and the organization.

There's more than one way to motivate an entire organization to perform at peak levels. In fact, according to Jon Katzenbach, author of *Peak Performance*, there are five ways – or balanced paths, as Katzenbach calls them.

The most successful organizations don't try to follow them all. They pick one or two paths and concentrate on excelling at them. They have ingenious recruitment methods for selecting people to match their chosen paths, and they continually reinforce the practices that lead to worker fulfilment along those paths.

The five paths, which Katzenbach identified through intensive research in high-performing organizations, are:

- *Mission, values and pride.* Katzenbach stresses that he's not talking about formal statements and company claims, but rather 'a current and recurring set of accomplishments that constitute a rich legacy that frontline employees can take pride in.'[4]
- *Process and metrics.* Employees know how their individual efforts contribute to the company's achievements. They know exactly what performance levels they are expected to achieve because they have had a say in what the measurements are and how they will be monitored. Rewards and penalties are directly related to performance against those measures, and employees 'constantly strive to achieve new levels of their individual best.'
- *Entrepreneurial spirit.* High risks and high rewards are the key here, and people who thrive in this atmosphere get a chance to share in the ownership of the company (both financially and psychologically). This is a path that works best for young, fast-developing enterprises, but it's hard to sustain when a company gets large.
- *Individual achievement.* Following this path, organizations provide plenty of opportunities for individual achievement and career growth. 'Individual roles are broadly defined and extensive efforts are made to equip each individual with the knowledge and skills required to fill these roles – and to move beyond them.' Both the individual achievement path and the entrepreneurial spirit path effectively tap into employees' self-interest.
- *Recognition and celebration.* Practised well, this path can work effectively when 'monetary rewards and incentives are constrained ... and the work

SMART PEOPLE
TO HAVE ON
YOUR SIDE:

JON R.
KATZENBACH

itself is seldom intrinsically interesting.' Southwest Airlines, for example, has followed it to phenomenal success. Katzenbach cautions that 'the celebrations must become an integral part of the management process, not a handful of random events.'

If five paths all work, how best can an organization choose which to take? Katzenbach offers this advice: 'First, get some knowledgeable group of managers to simply think about it – what we think works here and why. Then tap into the front line in some reasonable way, through focus groups and surveys, for example. Learn what's working and why and what the roadblocks are. You can identify that through management judgement and front line information. Start with what's already working.'[5]

Katzenbach advises beginning with just one path, focusing on getting it right, then adding a second path perhaps a year later. 'If you go with just one, it's pretty risky,' he warns. 'Some cases we looked at ran into really tough periods when one path wasn't providing enough of what the workforce needed at a particular point in time.'

But most of all, Katzenbach stresses the importance of *excelling* at the chosen path. He strongly advises against trying to be all things to all people. 'If you take a broad spectrum of everything we know about human relations, you're going to spend a lot of money doing it and at best end up being a better than average company, but not a truly outstanding company and not an outstanding motivator. You have to excel along something that is motivating to workers.'

Although the paths are different, says Katzenbach, one thing is common to them all – pride. 'What the best motivators do is instil pride. If you can tap into that you have a much better chance of motivating people than anything else you can use.'

Jon Katzenbach is the senior partner of Katzenbach Partners LLC, a New York City management consulting firm, and a popular speaker on teams, leadership and workforce performance. He is co-author of the best-selling book, *The Wisdom of Teams*. His also wrote *Teams at the Top* and co-authored *Real Change Leaders*.

- *Live the values of the organization*, establishing their own and the organization's credibility, serving as role models for everyone in the enterprise.

- *Demand fairness* in the treatment of all employees, customers and other stakeholders.

Ethics

Most people are basically honest. They pay tax. They confess when they lose a library book. If a cashier hands them extra change by mistake, they return it. And they trust that their employer is doing the same with the big money, big contracts and big opportunities. Assuming that, they take pride in the accomplishments and reputation of the organization for which they work.

Pride is a powerful motivator. Not only is that motivation shattered, it is replaced by a crushing sense of betrayal when employees find out that their trust in the ethics and honesty of the people for whom they work has been misplaced.

Smart quotes

'Enron issued a triple bottom line report, gave speeches at ethics conferences, and in 2000 won six environmental awards.'

BizEthics Buzz, July 2002[6]

It's a scenario that has made too many headlines recently, starting with the Enron debacle of autumn 2001. Those headlines have cast such a pall over business in general that it's not uncommon to hear people comment cynically – even bitterly – that the phrase 'business ethics' is an oxymoron. But cynicism doesn't stop people from longing to feel pride and trust again, to be confident that the satisfaction they feel in saying 'I work for XYZ Inc.' won't bounce back and smack them with tomorrow's headlines.

'So, what is business ethics? . . . it means making sound judgements between right and wrong, exercising the basic virtues of respect, dignity, kindness and courtesy in all manner of business, and working in the best interests of your clients. But, whether it's customer focus, vendor selection, employee relations, community service or all of these, business ethics is a set of un-bending principles that should guide your business operations and define your corporate image.'

Steven G Orluck, SVP, MONY Life Insurance Company[7]

SMART VOICES

Earning that trust takes more than speeches and engraved ethics statements. It requires organizational leaders to demonstrate honesty and integrity not only in the financial arena, but in areas like community service, the environment and the treatment of employees and customers.

Values

Speaking of Enron (such an easy target, unfortunately), *Harvard Business Review* reported that the company's corporate values, as listed in the company's 2000 annual report, included communication, respect, integrity and excellence. Even in an era of crumbled corporate icons, most companies haven't strayed as far as Enron did from its much-ballyhooed values statements. But it doesn't take a scandal-ridden corporate meltdown to disillusion and dishearten employees. As Patrick Lencioni said in the *Harvard Business Review* article, 'Most values statements are bland, toothless, or just plain dishonest. And far from being harmless, as some executives assume, they're often highly destructive. Empty values statements create cynical and dispirited employees, alienate customers, and undermine managerial credibility.'[8]

Conversely, honest and courageous values statements, scrupulously adhered to by management, hearten employees, attract and retain customers, and bolster management credibility. Actually, though, it's not so much the statements as the actions that count.

There's no one 'right' set of values. You'll find words like 'trust', 'integrity', 'teamwork' and 'empowerment' in many companies' lists. Surely they belong there, although they do sound a little like motherhood and apple pie. But the first time a corporate value jumped out at me was a few years ago when I found 'sense of urgency' among the printed Common Values of Caterpillar's Track-Type Tractors Division. That one felt different enough to have a little bite in it. The best values statements are an honest appraisal of the beliefs and attitudes that truly drive the organization's most productive practices. It's a lot more realistic to expect leaders and workers to practise such real values than fine-sounding ones that are at best wishful thinking and at worst deceptive platitudes.

Stated values are inspirational to employees only when they see the leaders in the organization model them, reward employees who practice them, and base systems and procedures like hiring, promoting, customer service and performance management upon them. In a *Harvard Business Review* article, Frederick F. Reichheld described how Scott Cook, founder of Intuit, the personal finance software firm, and his executive team lived their values when a crisis arose in 1995. Cook was on his way to a speaking engagement when he read in a newspaper about a bug in the company's tax preparation software. He called headquarters and told his executive team to handle the situation according to the company's core values, which included treating customers right, and total honesty and openness. Intuit offered a new copy of the software to any customer who requested it, with no proof of purchase required, and pledged to pay any penalties that the software users incurred due to the flaw. 'The pledge could have bankrupted the company,' Reichheld wrote. 'Intuit made the promise before the full extent of the problem was known.'[9] Just imagine how good employees felt about working for Intuit in the wake of that situation and how willing they would subsequently have been to go out of their way to satisfy customers.

> When the gap is large between stated values and leaders' behaviour, the best talent leaves when it can and becomes cynical when it feels stuck in a hypocritical enterprise.

Smart things to say about motivation

But, as inspiring as it is to see leaders model organizational values, it's demotivating in equal – even greater – proportion when leaders ignore them. Lencioni illustrated how demoralizing that can be in his story of a technology company that, with the agreement of the CEO, wrote collaboration into its new values statement. But a few weeks later, in an open meeting, the CEO scoffed at teams and stated that he believed achievement only occurred when people worked independently. A senior executive who left the company told Lencioni, 'The gap between what we were saying and what we were doing was just too great.'[10]

Fairness

What's fair? In truth, the familiar lament: 'It's just not fair!' often really means: 'I didn't get what I wanted.' But beyond individual disappointments, there's an issue of fairness that is broader, can be judged more objectively, and colours the credibility and esteem of organizations and their leaders. It also has significant impact on the motivation of individuals. It's affected by:

- *How consistent leaders are in their treatment of people across the organization.* Do people in one division have special privileges – days off, travel benefits, faster promotion track – than people in divisions with employees of equal experience and education?

- *How comparable wages and salaries are to those in other organizations* with similar products or services serving similar markets.

- *How comparable wages and salaries are among people within the organization* who have similar experience and are doing similar work.

- *How wide the range is between rewards for top executives and those for rank and file.* This is the era of extreme compensation for top execs. That's probably not going to change, despite well publicized cases where it hardly seemed deserved. But there's no doubt that employees do notice and they do resent it, especially in organizations with less than stellar financial performance.

- *How well people know in advance the standards against which their performance will be assessed* and reward decisions will be made.

- *How clear the criteria are on which all judgements are made* when there are winners and losers, e.g. the selection of a candidate for promotion.

- *How well the organization differentiates levels of performance.* Are top performers rewarded accordingly? Is there a real penalty for wilful poor performance? Is there help available for people who genuinely want to improve their performance?

The final bullet above raises the issue of discipline. In his research for *Peak Performance*, Jon Katzenbach was surprised at the role discipline played in top performing organizations. 'Frankly,' he wrote, 'we did not expect to find enforced discipline quite so important in higher-performing workforce situations. Some would argue that it is the antithesis of the empowerment notions that dominate the literature on energizing people ... For those who aspire to an emotionally committed workforce, discipline and empowerment must go hand in hand.'[11]

He described some examples of how discipline is enforced: at Southwest Airlines, candidates for flight attendants are dropped from the programme if they show up late for classes or ignore proper grooming. At Marriott, a bell captain explained the rules for proper treatment of customers and added, 'three strikes and you are out.'[12]

This is not the carrot-and-stick school of controlling behaviour, sometimes known as motivation through fear. This is about fairness, eliminating any complaint that, 'While I work my butt off, Joe doesn't do a thing and yet he gets treated the same as I do', which leads of course to the inevitable, 'So why should I put myself out?' It's also about clarity of expectations: 'I really blew it yesterday and nobody said anything. I guess they don't care whether we meet our goals or not.' This kind of discipline is neither punitive nor restricting; it's empowering.

> **KILLER QUESTIONS**
>
> If punishing mistakes is demotivating, how can discipline be motivating?

Leadership style

It's not just what leaders do that makes a difference in the motivation of an organization's employees, it's also *how* they do it. Both the prevailing style of leaders in an enterprise and their ability to flex that style to match various situations affect workers' enthusiasm, morale and willingness to do their utmost to meet the organization's needs.

There's a wealth of literature on leadership styles, and several different style taxonomies. One that is easy to relate to was developed by Daniel Goleman, the emotional intelligence guru. His model is based upon research by the consulting firm Hay/McBer, drawn from a database of worldwide executives. The model includes six styles, some of which have a more positive overall impact on employees, but all of which are effective in specific situations.

Goleman's six styles[13] are:

- *Coercive.* A do-what-I-say style of leadership that 'demands immediate compliance'. On the positive side, it's essential in times of crisis, but when overused (meaning any time but crisis) it leaves people feeling disrespected, erodes their sense or responsibility, undermines their feelings of ownership and destroys their accountability for their own performance. Impact on motivation: mostly negative.

SMART VOICES

Of Daniel Goleman's six leadership styles, the authoritative style works best most of the time, he says. But don't confuse authoritative with authoritarian.

- *Authoritative.* Sets the direction, then frees people to decide how to achieve it. Most of the time, this is the most effective leadership style, Goleman maintains, and it's especially effective when a business is adrift or a change is direction is needed. But it may not work if the team members are more experienced than the leader. In that case the leader may not have the credibility to pull it off. For the most part, though, the impact of this style on motivation is highly positive.

- *Affiliative.* 'Strives to keep employees happy and to create harmony among them.' Offers plenty of positive feedback and builds relationships with employees, fostering in them a sense of belonging and fierce loyalty. This style works particularly well when it is important to 'build team harmony, increase morale, improve communication, or repair broken trust'. However, affiliative leaders may ignore poor performance and offer little in the way of constructive feedback. While the overall impact of this style is positive, Goleman says it's most effective when combined with the authoritative approach – a dynamite combination for motivating employees.

- *Democratic.* Builds consensus. On the positive side, this style develops trust, commitment and ownership among employees. It also generates new ideas for pursuing the vision. The downside can be endless meetings and, when consensus is hard to reach, 'confused and leaderless' employees. The democratic style is less effective when employees are less than competent or inadequately informed. And it's a disaster in a crisis, when immediate decisions are essential. Overall, though, the impact of the democratic style on employee motivation is positive.

- *Pacesetting.* 'Sets high standards for performance' but gives little guidance for achieving them and replaces people who don't succeed. Although pacesetting can be effective with self-motivated, highly competent people, it often creates an atmosphere of fear that is devastating to morale. Goleman warns that pacesetting should be used sparingly.

- *Coaching.* Focuses primarily on developing employees. Coaching leaders give instruction and feedback, delegate and give challenging assignments. Their implicit message is that they believe in their employees and expect their best efforts. 'Employees very often rise to that challenge with their heart, mind and soul,' Goleman says. The style works great when employees want to improve, but less well when employees resist learning or the leader is an inept coach.

For leaders, the trick is to master each style and use it at the most appropriate time.

The view from the middle

If your slot in the managerial hierarchy is still a far distance from the ranks of top executives, you may wonder how you can enhance positive organizational effects and minimize negative ones among the people who report to you. You may not be able to change the direction of the entire enterprise or moderate an executive's abrasive style. But you can make a difference in your own work unit if you:

KILLER QUESTIONS

If I'm not part of upper management, how can I have an impact on the organization-wide motivational influences?

- Communicate the organization's vision in terms that relate directly to the work of your unit.

- Craft and communicate a vision for your unit that links to that of the organization as a whole. If you feel your organization lacks an enterprise-wide vision, then it's even more important to focus on defining a desirable future for your unit based upon your assessment of the opportunities and challenges your organization faces.

- Identify and communicate the values that drive ethical success in your unit. Live by them.

- Treat all your employees by the same set of well-defined standards.

- With the help of people who know you well, assess your own dominant leadership style. Use it wisely and apply other styles when they are more appropriate to the situation.

The smartest things in this chapter

- A credible, attractive vision energizes people to participate in its pursuit.

- Employees decipher organizational values more from the actions of management than from printed values statements.

- Leaders with high ethics, who model the company values and demonstrate fairness, inspire commitment among employees.

- Discipline (not punishment), combined with help for underperformers, convinces employees they are being treated fairly.

- Effective leaders are aware of their predominant style, use it appropriately, and know when circumstances require them to switch to a different approach.

Notes

1 Nanus, B. (1992) *Visionary Leadership*. Jossey-Bass, San Francisco, p.3.

2 Ibid, p.8.

3 For this and the three quotes that introduce the bullets that follow, see note 1, pp. 16–17.

4 Except where noted, the quotes in this profile are from: Katzenbach, J.R. (2000) *Peak Performance*. Harvard Business School Press, Boston, pp.29–46.

5   This quote and the succeeding ones in this profile are from a personal interview in the spring of 2002.

6   www.business-ethics.com.

7   From a speech given at Business Ethics Awards Dinner, November 1, 2001.

8   Lencioni, P.M. 'Make Your Values Mean Something' in *Harvard Business Review*, July 2002, p.113.

9   Reichheld, F.R. 'Lead for Loyalty' in *Harvard Business Review*, July–August 2001, p.77.

10 See note 8, p.116.

11 See note 4, pp.214–15.

12 See note 4, p.229.

13 The descriptions of the styles are based upon the article, 'Leadership That Gets Results' by Daniel Goleman in *Harvard Business Review*, March–April 2000, pp.78–90. The quotes are from *HBR OnPoint*, which includes a synopsis as well as the original article.

12
Winning Teams

Is it true teams have more fun? Absolutely. Well, not those ill-conceived groups of people forced together and told, 'You're a team now. Work together.' They don't have a good time. They're miserable most of the time. But a real team definitely has more fun and, in most situations, gets more done.

What's a real team?

The 'T' word covers a lot of territory. There are permanent teams, divided along functional or cross-functional lines. There are temporary teams, brought together to deliver one outcome, after which they disband. Most teams are small – some experts say 7–10 members is ideal – but there are examples of effective teams in the high double

Smart quotes

'In the rush to bestow the manifold blessings of teams upon our organizations, lots of things get called teams that probably should not be. The resulting groups are too big, too lumpy, *quite* mismatched, and more than a little confused. We call these assemblages mobs.'

Harvey Robbins & Michael Finley, *The New Why Teams Don't Work*[1]

digits (although they usually break up into small sub-teams for individual tasks or interim outputs). Team members may work side by side, but in this age of virtual everything, there are effective teams whose members are flung around the world, who communicate almost exclusively electronically.

But all these team variations share a set of attributes that differentiate them from other work groups.

- *Members have a common purpose and they need each other to attain it.* 'As we work to deadline,' said the leader of a team building a Web site for a research company, 'if any piece – any link – fails, we lose the chain.' The sense that others depend upon them and the discovery that they can depend upon others energizes team members to do their share and not let other team members down.

- *The team agrees on goals, tasks and standards for measuring success.* Most teams start with a defined purpose, but together the members determine how to achieve it.

Smart quotes

'Teams are more productive than groups that have no clear performance objectives because their members are committed to deliver tangible performance results.'

Jon Katzenbach and Douglas Smith, *The Wisdom of Teams*[2]

- *The team agrees on a working approach and rules of conduct* that cover meeting attendance, roles and responsibilities, decision making and handling conflict. Many teams begin by creating charters that spell how the team will make decisions, divide up the work, resolve conflict and conduct meetings. Charters aren't meant to be confining, but rather to be liberating, freeing members to focus on their tasks rather than struggling with constant logistical issues. To do that, they have to be living documents, so most teams revisit them periodically to ensure their continued applicability and to revise them if any clause outlives its use. (A charter that lies ignored in a drawer is worse than a waste of time. It's an invitation to cynicism.)

- *Members hold themselves accountable for team results.* This doesn't happen overnight. Putting it into a charter wouldn't ensure it either. It evolves. At first, people take responsibility only for their own tasks, and may point fingers if someone else misses a deadline. But as a team coalesces, that mind-set adjusts. The leader of one hi-tech team with a high-profile mission saw team members' attitude change from 'Someone's not doing what they're supposed to do,' to 'What can we do to help?'

With those factors in place, you've got a team. But does that really guarantee that team members will work hard and have a great time doing it?

It's a good start. But it's probably more realistic to say those characteristics are required but not always sufficient to assure team member motivation. Motivation gets a big boost when teams routinely follow certain practices.

Five habits of highly motivated teams

- *Allow members to express their opinions and ideas without fear.* Members encourage new ideas, respect even bizarre-sounding ones enough to hear them through, examine them thoughtfully and investigate their potential. This kind of behaviour makes a team fun, just the opposite of many a so-called team that's really a group of cowed or bored people dominated by one or two members who shoot down any ideas that are not their own. Any member who dares buck them gets branded – you guessed it – a poor team player. But it doesn't require such overtly hostile behaviour to subdue people. A smirk, a sideways glance, a brushed-aside suggestion – all of these do the trick. And after a few attempts, trying to contribute to such a group isn't any fun any more.

- *Seek input into a decision from everyone affected by it.* That's not just team members. It can mean customers, vendors, other departments in the organization. There's nothing that takes the enjoyment out of work like discovering too late that you missed one important piece of information and your efforts are for naught. Teams that seek out such news in time to avoid mistakes avoid such demotivating – and possibly catastrophic – events.

- *Encourage and reward innovation and change.* Teams are most often spawned by the need for change. (If it's business as usual you want, then methods as usual will achieve it.) That's what makes them exciting, even if it's also what makes them a little scary. Any team that falls victim to the 'We've never done it that way before' syndrome is almost certainly doomed to failure. In the best teams, members embrace new ways of doing things, and reward themselves with celebrations at each step along the way.

- *Air disagreements and conflict in the open*, focusing on creative solutions. Constantly smiling faces and nodding heads may indicate agreement, or they may signal groupthink or cover up smouldering resentment. So teams with plenty of energy and confidence provide forums for members to lay their differences on the table and work through them, often to a solution that is better than either side would otherwise have held out for. People who work out their differences respectfully often make the best allies, appreciating each other's contributions.

- *Spread leadership across the team.* Permanent work unit teams often have rotating leaders and project teams usually have assigned leaders

SMART VOICES

'Kirsten Machen of Chevron remembers being party to a clash of temperaments. "Two of us were at each other's throats ... What we did," she explains, "was figure out our main objective and make sure we focused on it." They both asked themselves what they were trying to accomplish. The answer for both of them was the same: build a portfolio. That required people thinking both long-term and short-term.'[3]

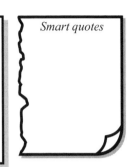

Smart quotes

'A recent study showed that fully 12 million people in 1997 received a mug imprinted with the words "There's no 'I' in team." A follow-up study found that 8 million of these recipients wanted to say: "No, but there's a 'ME.'" Among this group, 3 million actually *did* say it, and a quarter of these people went on to use their mugs to catch run-off grease from their gas grills. So the impact is not always what management intends.'

Tom Terez, BetterWorkplaceNow.com

accountable to upper management. But in teams that have evolved into mutual trust and confidence, practical leadership shifts, resting at any given time with the person best qualified to manage the task at hand.

In Western cultures, the best teams have another characteristic that drives their success: they recognize the importance and the crucial contributions of individuals. Teams aren't an amorphous mass of interchangeable bodies, marching in lock step. They are a group of individuals with unique talents who respect each other for their differences and take advantage of those differences to achieve a purpose that no one of them could accomplish alone – or even cloned.

And some habits of highly motivating team leaders

With more and more organizations using cross-functional project teams to pursue their goals, if you haven't already been called upon to lead such a team, you should expect it to happen soon. When it does, there are things you can do to ensure that every team member benefits from teams' potential for new experiences, growth and achievement.

- *Divide the creative work up so that everyone gets a piece of it.* By its very nature, project work is interesting. It's aimed at accomplishing something new; it's unpredictable because it hasn't been done before; it offers opportunities to work with people in other departments and other functions. But no project comes without its share of drudgery – the usual hundreds of phone calls, pages of letters and reports, hours spent in meetings rehashing the same issues, weeks of testing components, more weeks or months of meticulous rework. Your job is to ensure that all new members get shares of the good part, both to excite them and to inspire a sense of ownership.

- *Avoid depending too much on a few superstars*, while asking the regular folk to do all the back-up work. It's a common approach, but it risks burning out the top performers while turning off other team members. In the long run, the project will benefit from developing a wider group of contributors. And you may uncover a star in the making.

- *Empower team members* to determine for themselves how they will do their tasks – and to look constantly for better ways to do things.

- *Ask people what tasks outside their own specialities they would like to assist on.* It's a great way for them to learn something new.

- *Pair up people from different specialities* to work together on tasks that combine both sets of skills.

- *Rotate people among the project's tasks.* If your project lasts more than a couple of months, don't lock anyone into doing the same thing the whole time. When people switch jobs, it gives them a fresh start and brings a new perspective to each task that can move the project along.

- *Share the drudgery, too.* Instead of assigning one person to spend a week making phone calls, for example, bring in five people (including the prima donnas and yourself) to spend one day. Misery does love company.

- *Add fun to the humdrum.* Still using the phone call marathon as an example, give prizes for the most calls, most unsuccessful attempts to reach the same person, weirdest excuse for not answering – whatever inspires pride or laughter. Take periodic breaks to play.

- *Relate the routine to the final outcome.* This adds meaning to the task and makes it more palatable. Approaching one more phone call thinking, 'This is number 38 out of a hundred' is pretty discouraging. It helps to think, 'I'm getting one more piece of information that will help determine the market for our new product.'

- *Show your appreciation for each team member's contributions.* Do it often enough to be noticed, but not so often that it becomes white noise. Be very specific about what earned your appreciation, and about its contribution to the project. Most of all, be sincere. Appreciation is not a management technique, it's a sentiment. People who toss kudos around like tennis balls get pegged as phoneys very fast. The closer you stay in touch with the work people are doing, the more you'll find to be sincerely appreciative of.

- *Celebrate the team's accomplishments.* Mark each milestone with a party. Have cake and coffee or wine and cheese brought in just to tell people you appreciate how hard they are working on a particularly tough task.[4]

Silver bullet?

Are teams, then, a silver bullet, the answer to all your prayers for increasing motivation and improving performance? Not quite. In fact, while Jon Katzenbach, co-author of the seminal book, *The Wisdom of Teams*, touts teams for their power to motivate, he also advises caution.

'A real team,' he says, 'motivates itself. Team members tend to motivate one another around what they are doing and how they are doing it. If you get teams in the right places they are very motivational. But a lot of companies go into teams and create a lot of teams in a very undisciplined way. People don't know why they are doing it. They can't afford the time, they get tired of bonding, and they lose sight of what they are trying to accomplish. That can be very demotivating.

'If you go after teaming for purposes of motivation, you are likely to be disappointed,' he emphasizes. 'The only reason to use teams is to go after a performance objective.'[5]

But when you think about it, achieving a performance objective is why you want people to be motivated, isn't it? Chasing motivation without a performance objective in mind is working backwards for teams or individuals.

Even when you are in hot pursuit of a well-defined objective, teams aren't always the best way to go. Based on the advice of Robbins and Finley in their book, *The New Why Teams Don't Work*, here are recommendations for when to use teams and when not to:[6]

Teams surpass individuals when:

- *'The wider the input, the better the output.'* A great product idea, for example, can be improved upon with input from people who've made similar products and others who have made quite different ones but learned lessons that have broad application.

- *'The issue is cross-functional or multi-directional in nature.'* Whenever a project needs the co-operation of more than one work unit, a team is the way to go.

- *'The outcome/decision has potential high impact for department, division, or company.'* When it's really important, then you need the wider perspective, additional skills and synergism of a team.

Teams are more meddlesome than motivating when:

- *'Decisions are best made by one person.'* Sometimes you need a team to discover you've got an elephant and not a tree stump. But sometimes you really are dealing with a tree stump, and it only takes one person to arrange its removal. Bring in any more people and they'll just stand around wondering what they are there for.

- *'Decisions are predetermined.'* If management has made all the decisions in advance, then you don't need a team, you just need someone to make assignments and monitor progress.

- *'The outcome is not critical to company, division, or department success.'* Real teams are intense. You probably shouldn't waste that intensity on something trivial.

- *'Time is of the essence.'* Occasionally speed is more important than quality. When that's the case, assign your fastest working individuals. Team processes would slow them down.

- *'The project is either back-burner or of low priority.'* When the project is low priority, the team is doomed from the start since team members will be pulled away by other higher priority tasks. An experience like that only turns potential team champions into cynics.

It's true, teams may not solve all organizational problems. But for high quality, innovative outcomes, for opportunities to learn, and for the joy of participating in productive working relationships, teams surpass lone-wolf situations. And besides, teams do have more fun.

The smartest things in this chapter

- A group is a team when members have a common purpose and need each other to achieve it.

- In an effective team, members hold themselves individually accountable for team results.

- In motivated teams, members express themselves freely, seek wide input into decisions, and air conflicts openly.

- Practical team leadership shifts, resting with the person best qualified to manage the task or issue at hand.

- Effective team leaders ensure all members share both the creative work and the drudgery.

Notes

1   Robbins, H.A. & M. Finley (2000) *The New Why Teams Don't Work*. Berrett-Koehler, San Fransisco, p.123.

2   Katzenbach, J. & D.K. Smith (1993) *The Wisdom of Teams*. Harper-Business, New York, p.15.

3   Deeprose, D. (1998) *Recharge Your Team*. AMA, New York, p.46–7.

4   These suggestions are adapted from Deeprose, D. (2001) *Smart Things to Know About Managing Projects*. Capstone, Oxford.

5   From an interview in spring 2002.

6   See note 1, p.126.

13

Tactics for Tough Times

The United States Federal Reserve 'shifted yesterday from a neutral stance back to a worry over economic weakness', reported *The New York Times* on 14 August 2002. So it was official. The recession wasn't letting up. These were indeed tough times.

You might think that fear of losing their jobs would increase employees' motivation to prove they are outstanding workers who are worth retaining even if others are being let go. But fear doesn't work that way. Rather than prove their value with innovative work improvements, people desperate to hang on to their jobs often hunker down and do their tasks in the most conservative, risk-free manner possible. And that's the good news.

> KILLER QUESTIONS
>
> Why, when the company is in danger, do the employees seem unmotivated by any effort to save it?

The bad news is that, confronting the possibility of catastrophe, whole work units suffer anxiety paralysis.

Smart things
to say about
motivation

Unfortunately, many people have good reason to fear losing their jobs. The US Bureau of Labor reported more than 1,000,000 lay-offs in the United States in the first 6 months of 2002. While the numbers of workers losing their jobs edged downward from 2001 levels in both the United States and the United Kingdom, nobody in mid-2002 was feeling confident that the squeeze was over.

Even the best intentioned slow down, make mistakes, and generally spend more time worrying than working. More effort goes into analyzing the latest rumours than analyzing the newest production problems. Meanwhile, another group of workers blames their leaders for letting this situation happen, feels angry and betrayed, and may even retaliate, subtly sabotaging the leaders' attempts to rescue the organization from disaster.

Unless you work for Southwest Airlines (which has never had lay-offs), you're probably right if you think the first thing your company will do if it falls victim to the economy is cut staff. In fact, in good economic times or bad, the common wisdom for companies in trouble is that step one on the road to recovery is to reduce headcount. Companies that are not in trouble cut staff too, trying to inoculate themselves against future business threats.

However, while the most effective turnaround artists often wield heavy axes, they know that a crew of demoralized, demotivated survivors can drag down any recovery plan. So step two is to capture the energetic support of those who remain.

Advice from experts

Culled from the advice of several executives who have resuscitated near-dead companies, here is a list of must-dos to keep employees motivated when the road is bumpy and the destination uncertain.

When Dale Fuller became president and CEO of Inprise, as the software company Borland was known in 1999, he learned fast that the organization was in deep trouble. There was no strategy and no plans for new products. Fuller knew he had to come up with a product strategy fast, and he saw the potential for developing Internet and wireless applications, building on work the company had done in its more prosperous days. He called an all-hands meeting and told the 1100 employees, 'If you're working on a project that's not focused on the Net, you'd better figure out how to get it there quick, because over the next three months, I'm going to kill everything that isn't focused on the Net.'[1] To the product developers, it wasn't threatening, it was motivating. Finally they had a clear direction that built on the company's longtime strengths.

- *Clarify strategies and priorities.* 'One of the biggest signs that a company is in trouble is when the employees are confused about strategy and priorities,'[2] says Carlos Ghosn, a former Renault executive who nursed a dying Nissan back to health after Renault bought a controlling interest in the Japanese company in 1999. They may not buy right into your strategy – they've probably seen other strategies fail – but if your priorities are clear, they can begin to sort out their own, and that's energizing.

- *Communicate directly and physically.* 'Videoconferencing, telephone, e-mail, and other tools don't cut it,'[3] warns Eric Schmidt, who spearheaded the financial recovery of the networking software maker Novell in the late 1990s. To win the hearts and minds of employees, you have to show up in person, he stresses.

- *Make the survivors part of the solution.* Point the direction, and enlist them to determine what needs to be done to reach the goal, rather than impose decisions upon them. When Ghosn moved to Japan to become CEO of the struggling Nissan, he was not only new to the company, he was an outsider to the entire Japanese culture. 'I knew that if I tried to dictate changes from above, the effort would backfire, undermining morale and productivity ... I mobilized Nissan's own managers, through a set of cross-functional teams, to identify and spearhead the radical changes that had to be made.'[4]

Eric Schmidt also stresses that 'Smart people need to feel that they are part of the solution ... You tell them, "Look, I don't know how to solve this problem, so why don't you throw yourself at it and figure it out? Take the time and resources you need, and get it right."'[5]

- *Break through the culture of fear.* Easier said than done? Of course. But if you want more from your employees than nodding heads and turf protection, this is essential. As Schmidt says, 'In a culture of fear, which I think is a common condition in companies going through rough times, people are always worried about getting laid off, and so they suppress their feelings. Instead of complaining to their bosses, whom they fear might fire them, they complain vociferously to their peers ... [creating] a kind of pervasive bellyaching, a corporate cynicism.'[6] Schmidt tackled the problem at Novell by encouraging all employees to say what was really on their minds. He urged his staff to sit down every day with the people who report to them and ask how they are doing and if they are happy. He set an example by meeting frequently with groups of employees. Once, at a meeting with engineers he felt the atmosphere was too controlled. So he kept asking questions, pushing for answers until one engineer burst out with, 'Do I have permission to be passionate?' Schmidt explained, 'He'd been so constrained by the culture that he'd been afraid to promote his idea for fear of being shot down by his boss.'[7]

- *Create well-defined areas of responsibility.* Companies in trouble often shift responsibilities frequently as they look for solutions. After a while it's hard to figure out just what anyone is responsible for any more. So it's hard to get motivated to do anything. When he went to Nissan, Ghosn found managers whose responsibilities were poorly defined, plus a group of advisors 'doing little except undermining the authority of line manag-

SMART VOICES

LAUGHING THROUGH THE TOUGHEST TIMES

When skies are the darkest, laughter helps people stick it out. In a *Harvard Business Review* article, Katherine Hudson, CEO of Brady Corporation, recalled her days as head of the instant photography division at Kodak, which was fatally affected when a court ruled favourably for Polaroid in a patent dispute. She confronted the formidable task of keeping up morale while winding down the business. At a luncheon one of her managers gave her his old combat boots as a symbol of the challenge she faced. She donned them on the spot. Later she made a video to inform and boost the spirits of the sales force. It was a standard talking-head tape – until the end, when she got up and walked away, revealing her boots. 'It was gallows humor,' she wrote, 'but it helped keep people going.'[9]

ers.'[8] He put the advisors into positions with operational responsibilities and redefined the managers' roles so they knew exactly what their contributions to Nissan were. 'When something goes wrong,' he says, 'people now take responsibility for fixing it.'[10]

- *Hold everyone accountable:* Having responsibilities is one thing; living up to them is another. In companies on the brink of failure, there may be little incentive to do so, since nothing seems to help anyway. In a turnaround, that has got to change. When Mannie Jackson, a Honeywell executive who had once played for the Harlem Globetrotters, took over the helm of the fading Globetrotters organization in the early '90s, he found no one in the group was keeping an eye on its finances. 'I started holding everyone accountable,' he wrote in the *Harvard Business Review*. 'On Saturday, I gave people three things to do during the next week, and I gave out pens emblazoned with the motto "We do what we say we're going to do." Everyone had a pen, but if someone didn't come through, I took it away from them.'[11] The pens were a powerful symbol.

- *Reward accomplishments.* For Jackson, rewarding people for what they do is as crucial as holding them accountable for doing it. It's all part of what he calls creating a culture of accountability. He learned it, he says, from Ed Spencer, former CEO at Honeywell. 'When you hit a sales target, he threw a party for you and morale was very high as a result.'[12]

- *Keep raising the standards and expectations.* Once the turnaround begins, 'Don't be satisfied with last year's results,'[13] advises Jackson. Having tasted achievement, people will be motivated by new opportunities and the challenge to do even better.

No crisis, just constant change

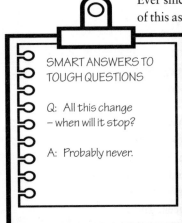

SMART ANSWERS TO
TOUGH QUESTIONS

Q: All this change
– when will it stop?

A: Probably never.

Ever since I saw the volumes on the shelves at Barnes and Noble, I think of this as the battle of the duelling book titles: *If It Ain't Broke, Break It*[14] vs. *Calling a Halt to Mindless Change*.[15] So far, the 'break it' philosophy is way out ahead. The slogan 'change is the only constant', which was a flash of paradoxical insight a dozen years ago, is a tired cliché now, but it's firmly entrenched in the mental operating manuals of most competitive organizations.

Entrenched or not, constant change creates constant tough times for many employees. You'd think they'd get used to it. But, if you are a manager, 'used to it' isn't really what you want of your employees. 'Used to it' suggests resignation, not motivation. What you want is for them to welcome change, thrive on it, be exhilarated and energized by it. Unless of course you are merely resigned to it yourself, just hoping to ride this one out. In that case, you need to examine your own motivation.

'There's an old story that when Adam and Eve left the Garden of Eden they said, "Now we're facing an age of transition." In fact, change has been a part of every age – railroad, TV, digitalization.'

Warren Bennis[16]

SMART VOICES

What keeps people – including you, perhaps – from embracing change? Some people might answer that with a question: why should anyone embrace change when it has such debilitating impacts and outcomes?

- *Change uproots people, both physically and psychologically.* Pack up and move again, folks. This group is moving down the hall or across town or maybe across the country. From office to cubicle to bull pen. What's next – a laptop and a corner in the cafeteria? Even if the new space is glorious, constant packing and unpacking and getting used to new surroundings is downright discombobulating. It's even worse when a work group is broken up and its members scattered. Then they have not only new physical space to contend with, but new co-workers too. Every reorganization has some reshuffling of people, with all the uncertainty that brings: What's my role in this group? What's my status? What's my relationship to this other person who seems to be doing what I used to do? Who can I turn to for help and comfort?

- *Change devalues the past* – at least that is how a lot of people perceive it. Goals you strove hard to achieve are cast aside. Were they the wrong goals? Results you were so proud of aren't going to be measured any more. Were you naive to care about them? Tasks you thought were important get eliminated. Does that mean they were really a waste of time before? For people whose sense of self-worth has been bound up with their work, these perceptions are confidence-shaking and saddening.

- *Change arouses fear of the unknown.* It starts when the first rumours leak out that another change is in the offing: the CEO is being replaced. Our department's being abolished. No, it's going to be absorbed into the new Division of Everlasting Confusion. We're merging with The Company from Hell and we're all going to report to Beelzebub. The big questions for each person are: Will I have a job? What will it be? Who will I report to? When the change is official, there is a new set of unknowns to unsettle people: What's expected of me in this job? Can I do it? What does it take to impress my new boss (or customers)? What if I fail? It's that last question that nags away, often unvoiced, until the individual has a good grip on the new job and earned some positive feedback – probably just in time for the next upheaval.

- *Change inspires cynicism* – especially when it happens over and over internally, but seems to have no discernible impact on the organization's financial results or even on its major product or service offerings. The typical response is 'Batten down the hatches, here we go again' or 'Been there, done that'. Except for the job uncertainty and discomfort they know they'll experience, employees would probably yawn. But it's no yawning matter when your job is at stake. So they protect themselves with a veil of cynicism while their respect for top management erodes and their trust in their leaders dissolves. They see that their managers are caught in the middle, trying to put a positive face on the situation while their own jobs are tenuous. Employees feel pity toward them. But that is not likely to inspire enthusiasm for the change and energy to make it work.

All that resistance takes its toll on change efforts, even turning expectations of failure into self-fulfilling prophecies. In her book, *This Isn't the Company I Joined*, Carol Kinsey Goman reports the results of two studies.[17] The first investigated why corporate restructuring failed, and the reason that popped up most often was employee resistance to change. The second study poses a possible explanation of that finding. It looked at employee attitudes about corporate change. Sixty-eight per cent of people queried didn't believe that management was open and honest with them. If you link the results of the two studies, you have to conclude that lack of trust in management has brought down many a change initiative.

What can you do to keep that from happening as your organization tunes up for its next big change effort? You can make change a motivator instead of a deterrent if you can convince people that:

- this change is worthwhile;

- this change builds on our strengths; and

- this change carries benefits for all of us.

This change is worthwhile

Especially in organizations that appear to be healthy, it's hard for employees to see the value of going through another disruptive change. To get their buy-in, you'll need to communicate clearly and convincingly that this effort really is worthwhile. Superficial answers won't do. You'll need compelling reasons. Look for them in:

- *The current business environment.* Can the economy support the strategy and goals you've been pursuing? Does the approach you've been pursuing respond optimally to the issues of globalization, technology advances and changing customer demands? Is your market still growing? If not, how do the proposed changes respond better to the current environment? If you can reveal hidden dangers lurking in a benign appearing situation, you can make a case for change. Convincing people

'One of the most effective strategies to convince employees to change when times are good utilizes proactive problem solving ("What are the future challenges that we need to begin preparing for today?") with status quo risk analysis ("What is the risk of trying to stay competitive in this dynamic business environment with the organizational status quo?").'

Carol Kinsey Goman, *This Isn't the Company I Joined*[18]

that, yes, the organization is doing swell but it could be doing even better, is tougher. You've got to be very careful not to give the impression that the enterprise is being greedy at its employees' expense.

- *The competition.* Is your market share shrinking? Is a competitor about to unveil a dramatic new product? Are your competitors providing service enhancements or discounts that threaten to dislodge your customers' loyalty? Facing news like this, people will galvanize into action, especially if you can show them that the plan to confront this competitive threat is credible.

- *The future.* OK, the present looks rosy, but what do future projections show? If you can build a credible case, based on expert analysis, for a need to prepare now to meet upcoming trends, you've got a chance of winning commitment from the people who will be implementing the changes your organization will need to move confidently into the future.

Building on strengths

For the most part, the trend toward wild diversification is over. If your appliance company is contemplating a major change, it's probably not going to be into sheep farming or anything equally far afield from your core competencies. When Fuller pushed Borland full throttle into Net applications, cutting off all non-Web related activities, he wasn't striking out into unknown territory. In earlier times, Borland had developed tools for distributed computing. 'The competitive competency was in the house,' he told *Fast Company*.

If you can demonstrate that the change your organization is embarking on will make even greater use of existing knowledge and skills, you'll boost the confidence and self-esteem of your employees rather than undermining them, as change so often does. If you involve employees in an assessment of current strengths and an analysis of their potential, you will get juices running for taking on new challenges.

Benefits for everybody

Well, let's be honest. It probably won't benefit everybody. It always happens that some people won't make the cut. What you can do for those people is be honest and help them find an appropriate place elsewhere in the organization or outside – someplace where they can use their existing skills and develop new ones. For those who will be around to make the change happen, there will be opportunities to tackle new challenges, learn new skills and work on new projects that will expand their knowledge and experience. While you are feeling your way in your own new job, it will be your responsibility to see to it that these opportunities occur and that people are recognized and rewarded for making the most of them.

Convincing the sceptics

Getting a crew of sceptical and fearful employees to buy into the benefits of change isn't easy. You'll have to do a lot of homework to pull together

> 'Proactive situations are those in which people seek to initiate change and, therefore, have more control over the process. Instead of being forced to change, they're motivated by a desire to do something new or differently.'
>
> Ken Hultman, *Making Change Irresistible*[19]

credible evidence. But you don't have to do it alone. In fact, you'll have more success if you don't. Instead of telling people all these good things about the upcoming change, enlist them to do the investigation. They'll buy into their own assessment faster than into yours, anyway. Point them in the direction of some good sources of information and encourage them to find the answers to these questions:

- What is there about our current business environment, our competitive situation, or our projected future that indicates we can't go on indefinitely as we are now?

- What competencies does the organization already possess that will form a foundation for successful change?

- What's in it for us? What new skills, experiences and knowledge can we expect to acquire?

- What should we be doing to become change leaders?

But what if you're not convinced either?

Worst case scenario. You did your homework and tried to find convincing answers to the questions above. But in your heart of hearts you don't think this change is worthwhile. In fact, you think a lot of people are going to be hurt with little gain. What do you do now?

Dedication to honesty doesn't require you to lay out all your fears to your employees. In fact, that would be disloyal and wouldn't win you any points from either side. But what you can do is lay out the situation:

- Here's what's going to happen.

- Here's what management hopes to achieve.

- Here are the obstacles that we'll need to overcome.

- Here are the best-case and worst-case outcomes.

Then enlist your work group in determining:

- What opportunities does this present for us?

- How can we take advantage of them?

- What are the potential pitfalls?

- What can we do to protect ourselves?

- What can we do to create a win for ourselves?

- What can we do to contribute to a win for the organization?

After your work unit has answered those questions, the change may not seem so damaging nor the people so helpless in its wake. In fact, both you and your employees will have a new purpose to spark your energy during trying times ahead.

The smartest things in this chapter

- When a company is in trouble, employees will mobilize to save it when they understand the strategy and priorities and have a say in how to achieve the goals.

- Constant change debilitates by uprooting people, devaluing their prior efforts and creating fear of what's to come.

- Employees will support change in good times when they are convinced it is worthwhile, builds on their strengths and benefits everyone.

- If you and your employees are sceptical, concentrate on potential opportunities and how to make the most of them.

Notes

1   Quoted in 'Borland Software: Back in the Black' by L. Tischer in *Fast Company*, July 2002, p.76.

2   Quoted in 'Nissan Motor Co.' by L. Tischer in *Fast Company*, July 2002, p.80.

3   Quoted in 'Novell's Eric Schmidt: Leading Through Rough Times' by B. Fryer in *Harvard Business Review*, May 2001, p.121.

4   Ghosn, C. 'Saving the Business Without Losing the Company' in *Harvard Business Review*, January 2002, p.38.

5   See note 3, p.120.

6   See note 3.

7   See note 3, p.119.

8   See note 4, p.40.

9   Hudson, K.M. 'Transforming a Conservative Company – One Laugh at a Time' in *Harvard Business Review*, July–August 2001, p.48.

10 See note 4, p.41.

11 Jackson, M. 'Bringing a Dying Brand Back to Life' in *Harvard Business Review*, May 2001, p.60.

12 Ibid.

13 Ibid.

14 Kriegel, R.J. and Patler, L. (1992) *If It Ain't Broke, Break It.* Warner, New York.

15 MacDonald, J. (1998) *Calling a Halt to Mindless Change.* AMACOM, New York.

16 From a 1998 interview with the author.

17 Goman, C.K. (1998) *'This Isn't the Company I Joined'*. Wiley, New York, p.108.

18 Ibid, p.120.

19 Hultman, K. (1998) *Making Change Irresistible*. Davies-Black, Palo Alto, CA, p.63.

Part IV

360-Degree Motivation, Centred on You

If your employees are struggling with a demotivating environment and jobs that don't turn them on, chances are you are, too. What can you do to charge your own batteries when nothing you do feels worth the effort? And what can you do when the people you report to or work with hold back their support, threatening your success?

Chapter 14 gives tips for stoking your own motivation in trying situations.

Chapter 15 offers advice for dealing with foot-dragging bosses, colleagues and customers.

14

Your Own Best Motivator

It's tempting to compress this chapter into one sentence that goes: read the previous chapters again, and everywhere you see the words 'employees' or 'workers', replace them with 'yourself'.

You've got the same needs, the same desires and the same occasionally immobilizing frustrations. All the things that will excite and invigorate the people who work for you will do the same for you. Some of those motivators you can actually give to yourself.

- Reward yourself when you've done what you know is a good job, by going out to a special dinner, for example. Take a friend along to keep reminding you of how great you are.

- When you need to be reminded of how important your work is, sit down and make a list of all the people who depend upon you and all the worthwhile outcomes to which you have contributed.

- When you feel your job is going nowhere, volunteer for a project that's quite different from your routine or take a course in something entirely new.

- When the organization you work for seems to be adrift, craft your own vision and seek out tasks that are relevant to it.

- When the atmosphere that surrounds you is charged with negativism, seek out the company of non-cynics. Every organization has some, and if you quell any thoughts of your own that they are naive, you'll be amazed at how much better you will feel in their presence.

Smart quotes

'When asked, most business-people say that passion – to lead, to serve the customer, to support a cause or a product – is what drives them. When that passion fades, they begin to question the meaning of their work.'

Richard Boyatis, Annie McKee & Daniel Goleman, *Harvard Business Review*[1]

Of course, it would be nice if you had a boss who would heed all the advice about motivating employees and apply it to you. But, in truth, motivation is internal. Others can change your external situation, giving your internal motivation some space in which to flower. But only you can search out the motivation within you and put it to work energizing yourself on the job.

This chapter focuses on ways to do that in situations that try the souls of working men and women. The subtitles below call these situations projects, but you can substitute the words job or task, and the message remains the same.

The dull and boring project

Groan. Your feet are dragging and your mind feels like it's right down there in the soles of your shoes being shuffled into this project. It's probably something you've done so many times before that you can barely tolerate thinking about it. But you are stuck with it so you'd better get started, you tell yourself – well, maybe after you check your e-mail, respond to that caller who's been leaving messages about changing your phone service provider, and make a list for grocery shopping on your way home.

OD consultant Karen Massoni remembers a project like that when she was on staff at a large financial services company. She and a colleague were assigned the task of developing 'yet another communication programme'. They met, grumbled a bit together, counted how many such programmes they'd created before, and wondered why they had to reinvent the wheel. 'This is so stupid,' they told each other. 'Where's the challenge?'

So they gave themselves a challenge. 'We decided to make it as creative as we possibly could,' Massoni recalls. They put all their energy into that. Suddenly they were having fun, and when it was ready to roll, the participants did too. 'What a fun way to learn!' one wrote on the evaluation form.

Smart quotes

'I happened on one of those online lists showing which wire-service articles have been e-mailed most frequently. The leader of the pack, by a great margin, was a Reuters article headlined "Boring, Passive Work May Hasten Death: Study." In the prior six hours, it had been e-mailed 870 times.'

Rob Walker, *The New York Times*[2]

Tips to motivate yourself

- Enlist a colleague or your employees, not because misery loves company but because you can bounce ideas off each other and it's more fun that way.

- Concentrate on being creative. You don't have to do things in the same old dull manner. Brainstorm more interesting approaches.

The impossible project

There are challenging assignments, and then there are assignments so daunting they look like a set-up for failure. It's hard to get motivated to work on a no-win project.

But maybe it's not impossible after all. In my mental book of life's lessons learned is a memory from my high school days in Edmonton, Canada. When I was a senior, I joined the school debating club. The topic my partner and I drew was based on legislation recently passed by our provincial government. When we saw the side of the debate we'd drawn, we were devastated. Although it had passed into law, it was a position that we all thought was stupid, a waste of money and nothing but grandstanding by the party in power. My friend, Barbara, and I couldn't think of a single good argument, and were convinced we hadn't a chance to win the debate.

I don't remember now how my math teacher found out about it, but he was the one who told me, 'Call your MLA [member of legislative assembly]'.

I was flabbergasted. 'You can do that?' I remember asking.

'Of course,' he replied. 'That's what he's there for. Go do it now.'

So I went directly to a school pay phone and called. I was put right through, and the MLA gave me all the arguments his party had used in parliament. Those arguments were very carefully crafted. To the surprise of our opponents, Barbara and I blew them out of the water. As far as I know, somewhere in the bowels of Victoria Composite High School there is still a big cup with our names engraved on its base.

Tips to motivate yourself

- Enlist the help of an expert when the task looks impossible. Somebody somewhere has probably done it before and is willing to tell you how.

- Even people who tackled similar tasks without success can be helpful. They can tell you the traps to avoid.

- Ask yourself: 'What can I learn by attempting this, even if the outcome isn't a big success?'

- Talk to the people who came up with the assignment in the first place. Why do they think this will work? What's their bottom line? If they were to do it themselves, where would they start?

The second best project

You hoped for a different assignment – one with higher profile, more prestige, or more priority perhaps – but you got stuck with second (or third) best. It's a big let-down.

The daughter of a good friend aspired to being a TV reporter. She came within taste of the job she wanted, then lost out in the final cut. So she took a position with a marketing company, definitely second best. But it did give her the opportunity to do infomercials and get on-camera experience and tapes to take on her next job hunt. Within a year, she moved on to become a television reporter in her state's capital.

> *Smart quotes*
>
> 'Avoid comparing yourself to others.
>
> When assessing your achievements, compare yourself to your past or your potential.'
>
> Sang H. Kim, *1001 Ways to Motivate Yourself and Others*[3]

Don't dwell on the superiority of the project you missed. The one you are stuck with probably has more potential than you think and, in some circles anyway, prestige that you aren't crediting it with. It may be disappointing to you, but you'll find plenty of people who think this assignment of yours is worthwhile. Let them convince you. Convince yourself to milk it for all it's worth.

Tips to motivate yourself

- Don't compare your project to the one that got away. Therein lies self-indulgent misery.

- Look for all the opportunities your new assignment offers for learning and showcasing skills. You may be able to turn it into a springboard for the next ideal assignment.

- Talk to the people to whom your assignment is important. You may get a new outlook on it. Even if they aren't the organizational superstars, they'll make you feel appreciated.

- Join a related professional association and introduce yourself as the person in charge of implementing XYZ in your organization. You'll be amazed at how many people think it's hot stuff.

- Make a list of all the people your assignment will have an impact on. Talk to them about how you can perform it in a way that gives them the most benefit.

- When you need a reason to give this project your all, think of those people.

- Boost your project's visibility by becoming your own public relations person. Call the editors of your company newsletter and suggest they do an article on it.

The dead end project

It's going nowhere and it's a waste of your time. Everyone thinks so. And as long as you keep thinking so, it's a self-fulfilling prophecy. To charge up your batteries, try looking at the project with a much broader lens.

For example, here's another chapter in my lesson book: in the early '80s, I was assigned to manage an experiment in computer learning that my employer was running in partnership with a technology company. The software was primarily for kids, and we worked with some local schools, letting their students come in to use the computers. But nobody else in the company seemed interested and after a while, the kids tapered down to a handful because in those days the public schools had no support capability for that kind of activity. So it wasn't a bad assignment, but it wasn't going anywhere and I was happy when my department hired a new person and my boss let me turn the whole thing over to her.

She approached it entirely differently. The technology didn't turn her on (she's a bit of a technophobe to this day), but she saw the broader potential

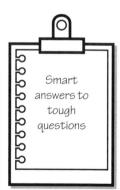

Smart answers to tough questions

Q: How can I break out of a dead end job without leaving it?

A: 'Look for problems to solve,' advises management consultant Joan Lloyd. 'For example, a bank teller saw the angst among her peers when they were expected to start cross-selling new financial products. She took the initiative and volunteered to create a training program for selling skills. It led her to a new job as a trainer.'[4]

and became head of a company-wide committee on self-directed learning in all forms. The committee stayed active even after the equipment went back to its makers. And my colleague got a departmental award.

Tips to motivate yourself

- Ask yourself: 'What potential does this project have that none of us has thought of?'

- Think outside your narrow goal and your technology to identify the broader purpose of your project. Promote that purpose to upper management.

- Find out who else within or outside your organization is working on a related project.

- Make contact with those people, and see what larger purpose you can accomplish together.

The thankless project

Somebody's got to do it. If it doesn't get done, somebody's going to be blamed. But doing it isn't going to win you any accolades. So, without much enthusiasm, you agree.

Martyrdom is such a pathetic motivator.

So don't fall victim to it. Stand up for your rights, not to escape the project or task, but to be properly recognized for it.

Tips to motivate yourself

- Put in writing all that goes into this project or task. If you haven't started it yet, draw up a plan of action with anticipated times. If you are already involved, keep a log. Present it to your boss or whoever is involved to demonstrate all that is involved.

- Negotiate. Ask for what you want in return. Compensatory time perhaps, if this project eats into your personal time or the time you need for your other work. At the very least, ask for recognition for your efforts: a letter to your boss's boss perhaps, copied to you of course. Or acknowledgement in front of your peers.

- Reward yourself. Establish milestones in the performance of this thankless project and reward yourself when you reach each one. Do it publicly to remind other people. Bring in a cake and share it, for example.

- Post a big calendar on your wall and mark off your progress in big symbols that no one who walks by can miss. When people ask you what it's about, tell them. If they don't ask, find a way to tell them anyway.

- This tip should be starred. If you are not doing this alone, if people reporting to you or your peers are in this with you, make sure they don't work thanklessly. Give them plenty of recognition. Have celebrations. Give fun prizes. Recognize and reward them until they are really charged up and you catch some of their fever.

When your world turns upside down

Kevin (not his real name) had his dream job. An organization development specialist, he worked for a large pharmaceutical firm in a cross-functional work group that brought together a variety of disciplines to manage change efforts, large and small, throughout the organization. He loved his responsibility for facilitating the people side of change; he loved the projects the group worked on; he loved the teamwork involved. Not least, he loved his new community, to which he had moved hundreds of miles from the city where he had lived most of his life.

Then came the merger, which Kevin and his colleagues refer to as the 'take-under', their way of suggesting the other merger partner came out on top. The other company had a dedicated organization development unit, headed up by a vice president who would have been out of a job under the set-up Kevin was used to. So Kevin had to move out of the cross-functional group and into the VP's organization.

'I ended up working with folks with a different world view,' Kevin says. 'My new boss told me, "I don't do all that touchy-feely stuff." He's very process-driven. He thinks process is the master; I think it's the servant. So he told me that if I wanted to be a more valued part of the organization, I'd have to become more process-knowledgeable.'

Smart quotes

'You will be bumping into some unexpected situations that weren't planned for … This ambiguity means that you will have to keep clarifying and reinventing your purpose as you meet these new circumstances.'

Kenneth Thomas, *Intrinsic Motivation at Work*[5]

Kevin had reached a point in his upside-down world where he really had three choices: accede, quit or fight. He thought about quitting. 'I was at a point of sending out resumés,' he recalls. But he didn't leave. Instead, he found a positive way to fight. 'I looked at what I did that was valuable to my clients,' he says, 'and I started being open to them about my need for their support. I asked people, to whom my work mattered, to make phone calls and send emails. I didn't generate a sudden flood. When someone made a positive comment to me about my work, I asked, "Will you please kick that upstairs?"'

As a result, he adds, 'Right now I'm almost untouchable because people in the businesses are saying they like the way I work.'

If you find yourself in a situation analogous to Kevin's, you have the same three choices he had. Actually, any one of them might turn out to be right for you. And just knowing you have options can make the situation more tolerable. To make the options real for you, follow the suggestions below.

Tips to motivate yourself

- Analyze the new situation very carefully. When you understand it thoroughly, it may turn out to be a change you can live with without betraying the work you want to do.

- Send out resumés. It will help you feel like you are taking control of your situation. You may even find a better job. Or you may discover the one you have looks pretty good in comparison.

- Line up your allies, as Kevin did, to give credibility to your preferred way to work. At the very least, it will boost your confidence (and give you good new words to put on that resumé if you need to).

The smartest things in this chapter

- When your work is boring, enlist a colleague and brainstorm ways to make it creative and fun.

- If the task looks impossible, seek out someone who has done it (or something like it) before.

- When you are stuck with a second-best assignment, use it to showcase your skills and learn new ones.

- When a project is going nowhere, connect with people doing related work and see what larger purpose you can accomplish.

- If your job changes dismally, line up all your ammunition before you decide whether to accede, quit, or fight.

Notes

1   Boyatis, R., A. McKee & D. Goleman 'Reawakening Your Passion for Work' in *Harvard Business Review*, April 2002, p.88.

2   Walker, R. 'Work Daze' in *The New York Times*, 23 June 2002.

3   Kim, S.H. (1996) *1001 Ways To Motivate Yourself and Others*. Turtle Press, Hartford, Connecticut, p.39.

4   Lloyd, J. 'How To Decide if Your Job Is a Dead End' 13 June 2001, www.JoanLloyd.com.

5   Thomas, K.W. (2000) *Intrinsic Motivation at Work*. Berrett-Koehler, San Francisco, p.75.

15
Upward and Outward

Can you see yourself in this scenario? You are psyched. You're revved up and ready to take on a heady new challenge. The people who report to you are as excited as you are. But your boss is hemming and hawing; peers whose support you need aren't fully committed; and you know you can't take your customers for granted.

You have some work to do or this enticing new project will die on the vine. If that happens, some of your own and your employees' enthusiasm for work will wither along with it. For your work unit to perform optimally, all the other stakeholders need to be motivated to support your efforts. Part of your job is generating enthusiasm and commitment among them.

KILLER QUESTIONS

What do I do if my boss is lukewarm about a project I'm working on?

About your boss

Before you begin a campaign to get your boss on board, ask yourself:

- Is it just this project my boss is reluctant to support?

- Does my boss usually support my colleagues' projects more enthusiastically than mine?

- Does my boss typically resist change and avoid making decisions in any situation?

Or, to put it more bluntly, what's the trouble here? Is it the project? Is it me? Is it my boss? How you tackle the problem depends upon your answer.

Smart quotes

'Motivating your boss means giving your boss reason to let you do your job the way you work best and giving you the chance to advance your career.'

Sang H. Kim, *1001 Ways to Motivate Yourself and Others*[1]

Support for a project

Let's assume that this foot-dragging on your manager's part isn't chronic, nor does it happen to you any more frequently than to your colleagues. It just seems to be this project your boss is hesitant about, despite its great potential (in your opinion). To win your boss over, prepare a well-documented presentation that covers these points:

- *How this project contributes to achieving the purpose and goals of the organization and the department* – especially its competitive advantages. In these tough times, your manager has limited budget and resources and can commit them only to ventures that he can defend to upper management. Make that easy for him.

- *How this project supports your manager's own goals.* If you think you know what your manager's goals are, it's a good idea to confirm them. If you don't know, make it your job to find out. Depending upon your relationship, ask about them in an informal discussion or be upfront and formal in your request and why you want to know: 'I'd like an opportunity to learn more about your goals and the direction you see this department headed so that I can align my efforts toward those objectives.' Then look for the links between those goals and the project you are promoting. If you have to make some project modifications to strengthen those links, it may be worth your while to do so.

- *How this project can fit into the budget and existing resources.* Do your homework and get your numbers right. Figure out how you could scale back if you have to, but save that for a last resort.

- *How the project will make your boss look good.* Be subtle, of course. Say 'the department' instead of 'you'. Use phrasing like: 'This will give the department an edge because ....,' 'This will be the first time the department has succeeded in ....,' or 'Top management has asked for ...., and no other department is doing anything that compares to this.'

- *People who have endorsed the project.* Whose support do you have? A highly regarded person somewhere else in the organization, perhaps, or a customer? Endorsements may give your project more credibility. If your boss's boss has said positive things, that's good, but be careful how you word that endorsement. You don't want it to look like you've gone over your manager's head unless your manager has sanctioned your doing so.

KILLER
QUESTIONS

My manager just authorized my colleague to fly first class to Hawaii to study Pacific bird migration and I can't get the same boss to sign a cab voucher for a trip across town to visit a client. What am I doing wrong?

Support for you

If you think your colleagues are getting more support from your manager than you are, you need to find out what they are doing differently. Don't assume your boss hates you or that your colleague is a 'teacher's pet'. More likely you are not making your case in a way that grabs your manager's attention and motivates a positive response.

Smart quotes

'Peter Drucker divides bosses into "listeners" and "readers."'

John Gabarro and John Kotter, *Harvard Business Review*[2]

All the points listed above under 'Support for a project' are equally important under this situation. In addition, improving your relationship with your boss is often a question of style and expectations. It's to your advantage to learn your manager's preferred working style and adjust to it. It's also up to you to identify what your boss expects of you and to fulfil those expectations. Look for evidence of:

- *Whether your boss is a listener or a reader.* Heed the advice in a classic *Harvard Business Review* article, 'Managing Your Boss': 'If your boss is a listener, you brief him or her in person, *then* follow it up with a memo. If your boss is a reader, you cover important items or proposals in a memo or report, *then* discuss them.'[3] Adjusting to your boss's style is often a question of how you present the details. A listener is going to want to hear a lot of them, so be prepared to verbally present a cogent, well-documented argument. Your follow-up memo is confirmation and a tool your manager can use to carry your case forward. If your manager is a reader you'll see eyes glazing over if you say more than the key points.

But be prepared – a reader-manager who has read your proposal in advance may have plenty of questions.

- *How much background information your boss needs to feel comfortable.* It's not just listener/reader differences that guide your presentation of detail. Pay close attention to whether lots of information gets your boss involved or fidgety. If you haven't figured that out yet, organize your written reports with your main points and your recommendations up front, followed up by all the background information any data-fiend could want. Start your presentations pretty spare and hard-hitting, but with lots of invitations for your boss to break in and ask questions (and have the answers ready). As you catch on to what works, plan your presentations to your boss's precise need for detail.

- *Whether your boss needs to be intensely involved or is a delegator.* You can keep a high-involvement boss happy and stave off the worst micro-management if you take the initiative to inform him frequently of what's going on with your projects. But delegators need to be kept informed too, for their protection and yours (in case something goes wrong) and so you can get feedback. So even if your boss is leaving you alone, touch base with her regularly with the highlights.

- *How your boss expects you to handle problems.* Clarify with your boss what kinds of problems you should take right to him, which ones you should solve yourself but inform him of, and which you should just handle alone.

- *What your boss expects concerning completion dates and milestones.* Are deadlines sacrosanct or guidelines? If you think the main purpose of a good plan is to change it, and your boss thinks due dates are carved in stone, you may be driving her crazy while blithely ignoring her warning signals. You'll help your cause by meeting her expectations or giving her good reasons well in advance of slipped dates.

Support for the department

There are managers out there who are burned out, too frightened to move, suffering in a job that's wrong for them or just not very ambitious (making you wonder how they got where they are). Lighting a fire under one of these can be such an impossible task that some advisors suggest that you stop trying to 'fix' such a boss and grab every opportunity to fill in the gap your boss leaves in the organization – giving your boss credit and making him look good in the process. Why? For the experience. It's a great opportunity to do high-level work way before you'd get the chance if you waited to move up the ladder.

Of course, that doesn't always work either. A do-nothing boss may be so firmly entrenched that you can't get around him to take charge of your own actions and move forward. But before you throw up your hands and quit – either mentally or physically – you probably want to at least try to rev him up a little. Here are some steps to take.

- *First, remember it is possible that, when you think your boss is just being recalcitrant, she actually knows something you don't* that makes caution the best choice of action. So prod a little: 'Why do you think this is a bad move?' 'What negative outcomes are you concerned about?' Even: 'Is there something you must keep confidential that makes this a poor choice of action?' If the

Smart quotes

'Does your boss run from any decision that might create risk or conflict? Then "work" him by assuaging his concerns ahead of time. Don't present an idea without a list of people you know will support it. And give him concrete strategies for how you'll handle any unavoidable conflicts.'

Bob Rosner, *Managing Your Manager: How to Overcome Your Boss Blues*[4] answers are vague, see what you can learn from people in other parts of the organization or elsewhere in the industry.

- *To make sure you are stating your case as powerfully as you can, revisit all the points under 'Support for the programme' and 'Support for you'.* Especially if your boss is new, it's possible that neither you nor her other direct reports are reading her style yet.

- *Get to know the pressures your boss is operating under.* Maybe he's being judged on his ability to keep costs down. Maybe his boss is afraid of risk. Maybe there's a threat that his department will be pulled out from under him. When you pitch a proposal, think about how it will mitigate those pressures.

- *Assess your boss's strengths and weaknesses.* Recognize her strengths. Bosses need recognition too. Show her how your proposal would use them to the advantage of the organization, herself and your project. If you have a strength that compensates for areas where she feels less secure, offer to support her (not just on your project), even taking over some tasks she finds onerous.

- *Be enthusiastic about your work and the projects you envision.* Talk about how important you think they are. Excitement is contagious. Your boss might catch it.

Energizing your colleagues

So much work is cross-functional that you almost certainly need the co-operation of colleagues in other departments to move your projects along to fruition. What with other priorities, other work pressures and trying to pursue their own agendas, they may not always be motivated to devote their all to the things you deem most important. Excitement may be contagious, but you'll probably have to coax them out of quarantine if you want them to catch it.

To win their commitment and spur their participation, here are actions to take:

SMART ANSWERS TO TOUGH QUESTIONS

Q: What can I offer people who don't report to me to get their co-operation on my projects?

A: Relationships, opportunities, being in on the action, recognition.

• *Build a network of relationships throughout your organization* before you need your colleagues' support, expertise or pairs of hands. People who know you, respect you, even owe you a few favours will commit time and resources to you more willingly than people who are unfamiliar with you and don't know your track record of success.

• *Be prepared to answer 'What's in it for me?'* – whether anyone overtly asks it or not. Figure out how your project will benefit those you want to lure into it. Are you creating a product or service that will make their jobs easier? Developing a new process that will save everyone time? You'll have more success getting their co-operation if you can relate your undertaking to their needs.

• *Involve them in goal-setting.* If you need the help of others on a project, invite them to participate in establishing the specifics of the final outcome and the milestones along the way. You'll get more buy-in and enthusiasm from people who have a say in determining the deliverables and how to achieve them.

• *Offer people opportunities to showcase skills* they may be underutilizing or to learn new ones they'd like to add to their repertoire. Being able to build and demonstrate competencies is a big motivator for many people.

- *Go for consensus* when there are decisions that affect everyone, unless it's an emergency. If you are not experienced at leading a team decision-making session, bring in a skilled facilitator.

- *Make a list of everyone who is going to be affected by your project* – those who will benefit and those who will be inconvenienced by it. Keep them all informed of project progress, both the good news and the bad.

- *Don't place blame* when things go wrong. Although you may need to discover the cause of a failure to be sure it doesn't happen again, treat it as a learning experience. Using phrasing such as, 'Since doing ABC led to XYZ outcome, we need to be sure we don't do that again. So let's figure out what to do differently.' That's a lot more motivating than pointing fingers at one person to get the rest of you off the hook.

- *Make sure everyone gets proper recognition*, both for individual contributions and for the success of the entire undertaking.

Convincing your peers to support your projects is a little like going to a swap meet. You have to offer something in return. It's never too soon to make offers. Even before you need their help, offer yours generously to support their operations. Although the routes are sometimes roundabout, favours do find their way back.

Smart quotes

'That man is a success … who looked for the best in others and gave the best he had.'

Robert Louis Stevenson

Customers – the ultimate stakeholders

Everybody has customers – whether down the hall, across the country or around the world. Unless somebody wants your output, you're out of business. Keeping customers motivated to use your product or service and to continue to choose it over your competitors' is a responsibility you can't escape.

10 hot tips for motivating customers

1   *Treat customer interactions as relationships, not transactions.* Keep those relationships alive by touching base with them regularly. Ask them to describe how they use your product or service and what you could do to make it even more useful.

2   *Show customers respect.* Keep appointments. Be on time. Learn as much about their products or services as they know about yours. Be there when they need you.

3   *Listen more than you talk.* The less time we spend talking, the more time we have to learn about the customer's immediate and broader needs. Responding to those broader needs can make us invaluable.

4   *Be alert to each customer's style.* Does he enjoy fellowship or appreciate efficiency? Does she need to know the *why* and *how* behind everything or is she interested solely in *what* you offer and *what* she needs to do to benefit from it? Is he looking for a partnership or a hands-off transaction? What turns on one customer may leave another gasping for air.

5   *Be as clear upfront about what you can't do as you are about what you can.* Vagueness early on can lead to confusion and a breakdown of trust later.

6   *Promise extras, and always fulfil your promises.* Small personalized extras like books, magazine articles or gadgets related to your customer's needs demonstrate your insight and your commitment.

7   *Follow up after delivery.* You've got to keep working at a customer relationship, just like a marriage. The delivery is only the wedding.

All the work comes afterward. If you want to celebrate anniversaries, you've got to keep the romance alive.

8   *Solve problems the first time they are brought to your attention.* Don't make a customer tell you twice that something is wrong. Problems are great opportunities for developing relationships. Studies show that solving customer problems leads to higher satisfaction ratings than providing something that never causes a moment of trouble. (But it's probably not a good idea to build in glitches just so you can be a super-saviour later.)

9   *Never blame someone else for a problem – whatever its cause.* Blaming someone else simply undermines the customer's trust in you and confidence in your entire organization. Instead, do your customer and yourself a favour by becoming the champion for solving the problem, wherever it occurred.

10   *Don't use 'policy' as an excuse for not meeting a customer's needs.* No customer wants to do business with an organization that has outmoded, rigid policies. Do your homework; then make an economically sound case for changing any policy that goes against your customer's legitimate interests. Enlist all the high-powered support you can get to influence the decision makers. If you can't get it changed or your homework reveals the policy isn't so dumb after all, then it's your job to develop an alternate way to meet the customer's end goals.

That's it then – 360-degree motivation, with you in the middle and your employees, your boss, your colleagues and customers all around. If all of you take pride in what you do, get some pleasure from the doing and recognize each other for your efforts, that's enough motivation to keep the wheels of commerce turning, the arts world creating and the sciences continually inventing.

What's left? Motivating your kids, perhaps, to tidy their rooms and do their homework. But that's a topic for a different book.

The smartest things in this chapter

- To win your boss's support for a specific project, relate your proposal to organizational, departmental, and her own goals.

- If you feel you never get the support you deserve, identify your boss's style and expectations and adjust to them.

- If you work for a boss who consistently avoids decision making and risk taking, pitch your project proposal to mitigate his pressures and mollify his fears.

- To get your colleagues' support, answer their question: 'What's in it for me?'

- Treat customer interactions as relationships, not transactions.

Notes

1   Kim, S.H. (1996) *1001 Ways to Motivate Yourself and Others*. Turtle Press, Hartford, CT, p.43.

2   Gabarro, J.J. & J.P. Kotter 'Managing Your Boss' in *Harvard Business Review*, May–June 1993, p.155.

3   Ibid.

4   Rosner, B. (2000) *Managing Your Manager: How to Overcome Your Boss Blues*. Working Wounded/Retention Evangelist.com.

Index